THE PRACTICE OF MEDITATION

Explains the objective, subjective and subconscious layers of the human brain, and gives a fourfold exercise in the practice of meditation. This is based on yoga principles of posture and breathing and includes a detailed thought-sequence to accompany the physical routine.

I0656647

Other titles in the series
THE ANCIENT ART OF OCCULT HEALING
CANDLE BURNING
COLOUR HEALING
DOWSING
DREAMS
GRAPHOLOGY
HOW TO DEVELOP CLAIRVOYANCE
HOW TO DEVELOP PSYCHOMETRY
HOW TO READ THE AURA
HOW TO UNDERSTAND THE TAROT
INCENSE
INTRODUCTION TO THE CHAKRAS
INTRODUCTION TO THE I CHING
INTRODUCTION TO THE MYSTICAL QABALAH
INTRODUCTION TO TELEPATHY
THE MAGIC OF THE RUNES
NUMEROLOGY
OCCULT EXERCISES AND PRACTICES
THE OCCULT PROPERTIES OF HERBS AND PLANTS
PALMISTRY
PRACTICAL TIME TRAVEL
THE PRACTICE OF RITUAL MAGIC
PRECIOUS STONES
THE PSYCHIC POWER OF HYPNOSIS
PSYCHOSOMATIC YOGA
REINCARNATION
THE THEORY AND PRACTICE OF ASTRAL PROJECTION
TRANSCENDENTAL MEDITATION

THE PRACTICE OF MEDITATION

by

CHARLES BOWNESS

THE AQUARIAN PRESS
Wellingborough, Northamptonshire

First published 1971
Fifth Impression 1976
Second Edition, revised, enlarged and reset, 1979
Second Impression 1981
Third Impression 1983

© CHARLES BOWNESS 1979

This book is sold subject to the condition that it shall not, by way of trade or otherwise, be lent, re-sold, hired out, or otherwise circulated without the publisher's prior consent in any form of binding or cover other than that in which it is published and without a similar condition including this condition being imposed on the subsequent purchaser.

ISBN 0 85030 182 3

Printed and bound in Great Britain by
Richard Clay (The Chaucer Press) Ltd.,
Bungay, Suffolk.

CONTENTS

Beyond the confines of the mind, say the mystics, lie states of consciousness that can transform the man into saint or sage. But to reach such exalted states, self must be left far behind, for self is built of impermanent constituents. Meditation is the method of awakening one's mind to a knowledge of levels of consciousness beyond those habitual to it.

CHAPTER ONE

WHY MEDITATE?

When you realize that you can alter yourself in any way you want, given the knowledge and patience, the next question is one that insults some people: 'Do you know what you really want?' Many people take a second-hand estimate of happiness, and are not really happy even when for a moment or two they think they are.

Life at the ordinary level is largely a chain of repetitive appetites. We wish for something and try to gain it. Then a new desire arises and again we chase fulfilment or satisfaction. But the fulfilment or the satisfaction turns out to be only temporary.

Everything thought and done up to the present moment is a cause for future effect. In other words each life is the cause of much of its own destiny. Yet even the power of the past is not irrevocable. Are you content to be merely an embodied hunger, whether your hunger is an aching for the more obvious forms of foolishness, or for higher things?

Of course you are not content.

Compulsions of Everyday Life

Self-knowledge can give freedom and provide principles on which to found true judgement. What is generally called meditation provides the insight into one's own character necessary to self-reliance. Most of the compulsions of everyday life may well be socially respectable, yet are often neurotic in origin because they are the result of the tyranny of opinions.

The processes of meditation can eradicate such tyranny and teach a person to stand on his own feet. Lack of mental control is as damaging to the personality as lack of physical control is damaging to the body.

Each person is responsible to himself for his own actions, and if he is incapable of self-discipline the results are obvious. These results may not appear to seriously affect others, but a badly organized mind is always ultimately harmful, to its possessor at least.

The harm done on the general social level may be evident in that the person concerned is regarded as weak, foolish, silly, and of little consequence. There is no need to elaborate on the disadvantages of such a reputation.

Yet if a person develops his mind, training it to obey his will, then such a person is noted for reliability, strength of character, and outstanding qualities such as a retentive memory, an ability to absorb knowledge, and also the ability to utilize such knowledge when necessary. In this case, there is no need to elaborate on the advantages of having such a personality.

Meditation Reveals Wisdom

Beyond the mundane social advantages to be gained are those in the spiritual sphere. Meditation is known to all the major religions and philosophies. It can be applied equally by the atheist and the religiously inclined to throw a light into the hidden aspects of the mind to discover the truth of wisdom inherent in all beings.

Most of us indulge in fears and worries. Meditation shows you what is superficial and what is important. You can then eliminate or ignore the former and deal with the latter. Gradually life becomes guided by principles of right action and not by moods of the moment.

If a man misses his train it is useless as well as harmful to fly into a temper. The causes must be considered, and that which needs putting right must be put right, whether it is the clock or the man himself.

Unpleasant facts may be ignored until forced upon the notice by inescapable experience. Better to face them calmly and wisely, and then something helpful can be done to ease or control the situation.

Right Action
Everyone is aware of the benefits of physical training, but a good physique is ill-matched if accompanied by a weak intellect. We are not merely bodies, we also possess a mind. If that mind is untrained, little used, or wrongly used, then we are not living fully. Envy of someone else's intellect has no practical result, and to express envy is to look foolish. Qualities in other people which are worth emulating can be acquired by one's own right action.

Each bad quality can be tackled and reformed into something useful, admirable, dynamic. It is an interesting and exciting task. The mind training of meditation is the key to self-mastery and that contentment which is lasting happiness.

CHAPTER TWO

WORKSHOP OF THE MIND

The term 'unconscious', now so familiar to all readers of modern works on psychology, need not be supposed to have any special mystery about it. For it is no new abstraction, but is simply a collective word to include all the seemingly forgotten experiences and impressions of the past which continue to influence our reflections and desires and conduct.

What most of us can remember at any time is

only a little part of what has happened to us in the past. Yet we could not remember anything unless we 'forgot' almost everything. The brain is an organ of forgetfulness as well as of memory. Also, we tend to become unaware of many things to which we are thoroughly accustomed. Force of habit blinds us to their existence.

The Great Discovery

It is this 'forgotten' and 'habitual' that makes up a great part of the 'unconscious'. If we are to fully understand ourselves, our conduct, and our reasoning, and if we wish to aspire to guide our lives and relationships more happily, then we cannot neglect the great discovery. We must accustom ourselves to novel (and to some people) revolutionary conceptions of the mind.

We have to learn to consider the mind as conscious knowledge and intelligence, as what we know and our attitude to knowing. We must discover our disposition to increase our information about ourselves, and our ability to classify that information, assess it, criticize it, and apply it.

We do not think enough about thinking, and much of our confusion arises through the illusions we have held for years. The first thing we notice about thought is that it moves with incredible rapidity. So quickly does one thought follow upon another that it seems impossible to arrest the process long enough to have a look at one single thought.

If someone makes the old bargain offer to us of 'a penny for our thoughts', we always find that not only have we a vast selection of thoughts to offer, but also that the request itself has set up an entirely new train of thought concerned with selecting! Few of us choose to offer the original sample of spontaneous thinking, being frequently slightly ashamed to expose the trivial nature of it.

Alternatively, we may feel that such thought is too personally intimate, or even ignoble, to be revealed. Many people suffer occasionally from a kind of guilt in finding it difficult to believe that for much of the time other people's thoughts are as silly or trivial as their own. There is little need to worry about this, for they probably are.

Reverie

If we are not engaged in some task requiring concentration, our thinking assumes the form of reverie. Reverie is spontaneous and undirected, its dictionary definition being 'to dream', 'a state of musing' and so on. This kind of thinking is our favourite kind, because we can be self-indulgent about it. Its course is determined by our resentments, our likes *or* dislikes, our desires and their frustration or fulfilment.

Ideas take shape around our own egotism. The free association of ideas in a reverie is a guide to our fundamental character. Such loose reflection of our personal nature is of course conditioned by a complexity of hidden or forgotten experiences.

It can be readily seen that the mass of prejudices and the lack of direction involved in the reverie can be a powerful enemy to any other kind of thinking. Such egotistical speculation has a strong tendency to self-justification which can, through persistent habit, form a barrier to honest, detached increase of knowledge.

Practical Decisions

Although most people spend much of their time indulging in reverie, the reverie is frequently broken by the necessity of having to make practical decisions. Such necessity may be simple, like deciding what to have for lunch, or it may be more serious, like deciding to go after another job, or to invest some money, or to leave home.

Decision making can easily be distinguished from reverie, and is therefore a different kind of thinking. Some decisions may be made impulsively, others may be arrived at only after much careful thought and the weighty pondering of relevant facts.

In the case of most people however, it is true to say that the need to make decisions is often resented. We find it difficult to 'come down to earth', to 'get our feet on the ground', to have to 'make up our minds'. It seems much more pleasant to live in reverie, and leave the decisions to someone else. This feeling, in part, is why few are leaders and many are led.

CHAPTER THREE

POWER OF REASON

Naturally, we all like to consider ourselves as reasonable people. Yet on many issues we are unbelievably careless in the formation of our beliefs and opinions. When what we imagine to be our firm belief is challenged we often defend it passionately. But do many of us pause to reflect that what we may be defending is not the idea or belief so much as our own self-esteem?

It is in the nature of the majority of us to stubbornly defend ourselves against what we feel to be an attack. In this way we tend to regard our ideas, beliefs or opinions as personal property to be defended as we might defend tangible property such as our homes or other material possessions.

Mystique of Persuasion
This is not to suppose that our ideas are not subject to change. They can be stimulated, modified, and

altered by the subtle mystique of persuasion. Orators, advertisers, and public media purveyors know this well.

An appeal to convictions underlying our superficial or conscious thought can direct our thinking into almost any channel, where a direct frontal challenge would fail.

Lots of people never take the trouble to examine the origins of their opinions, and the result is that what they imagine to be their reason at work is merely the finding of arguments to enable them to go on believing as they already do. We can all find 'good' reasons for what we think, do, or believe, but how many of us can find 'real' reasons?

Preconceived Notions
Usually the 'real' reasons for being as we are, are as hidden from ourselves as they are from others. And so, in many aspects of our lives we are the result of preconceived notions, emotion, prejudice, and even ignorance.

Having adopted many of the group ideas from our environment, unconsciously absorbing them through the persistence of suggestion, we cling tenaciously to them.

Since the group feeling is tenacious, it would be foolish to go about displaying scepticism on every occasion, because this would only invite disapproval, contempt, or condemnation. And in any case, if we challenge the opinions of others we must at least have the ability to present our own case in a rational and truly reasoned manner.

We cannot challenge any 'reason' without first challenging and discovering our own 'reason'.

Resentments
Even the greatest of men can be sensitive about their reasoning being challenged or criticized, for

we are all subject to resentments. But the great man, from the commonplace premise of having a 'bee in his bonnet', can often transmute his self-defence into something more than wounded pride.

This ability to rationalize experience has resulted in works of genius being produced. A sublimated grouse or aversion has frequently had an ultimate outcome in painting, music, literature, or other fields of activity. The genius has been able to overcome restrictions and to utilize his own experience in a high form of self-expression. This ability is what makes him great.

So instead of going about with a permanent grudge, or the all too common 'chip on the shoulder' of envy and angry resentment, it would obviously be so much better if we could channel and direct all that wasted energy into some useful form of activity or thought.

CHAPTER FOUR

CREATIVE THOUGHT

If one were to ask someone else what creative thought meant, the answer might well include the word reason. But as we have already seen that what is regarded as reason is frequently fallacious, I have preferred to use here the term 'creative thought' for the analytical power of the mind.

Creative thought has nothing to do with reverie, for it is not concerned with our personal humiliations or our complacencies. Nor is it directly concerned with our having to make decisions. It is not the defending of our cherished prejudices.

Creative thinking is a higher aspect of thought because it is that power of mind which can lead us to a change of mind. It is the kind of thinking that has gradually evolved the world of men from savagery and squalid ignorance into the degree of comfort and knowledge now enjoyed. Not all men evolve equally or at the same time however. The world is not populated by a super species of human beings.

A Matter of Degree
The faculties which go to producing a Shakespeare, a Beethoven, a Galileo, or a Faraday are faculties we all possess. But it is a matter of degree.

What distinguishes the genius from the ordinary man is an intense curiosity plus an urge to express or create.

The curiosity is real and activated, not merely idle. Inevitably, that which is discovered by means of this curiosity must realize itself, that is, be expressed.

We all have a basic curiosity, but for the most part it is secondary, such as the unimportant curiosity promoted by newspapers as to whether the actress will get divorced or not.

There are times however, when we find ourselves indulging in a mood of what might be called 'pure curiosity'. This is the time when we are not preoccupied by personal feeling or reverie. We catch ourselves in the act of observing things and making reflections about them which have nothing to do with our usual thoughts.

Pure Inquiry
This spirit of pure inquiry is that possessed to an intense degree by the genius. When Galileo saw the lamps swinging in the ceiling of the cathedral, he could not have been the only person to have observed them. Newton was not the first man ever to see an apple fall from a tree.

But most observations do not necessarily result in

real creative thoughts arising. The ideas which the observation may create must be utilized, reconsidered at some future time and applied, for that to happen. To observe things while conditioned by reverie is to lose the potential value of observation.

The remarkable creation of Sherlock Holmes by Sir Arthur Conan Doyle showed us the author's own ability for observation expressed through the medium of a fictional detective. A Holmes would not simply see a 'nice' room when he entered it, but would recognize the intrinsic quality of it and deduce the character of its occupant.

Miscellaneous Observations

The curiosity of many people for much of the time is diluted by the personal preoccupations of reverie, so that they collect plenty of miscellaneous observations, but have little power to use them for any definite purpose. Even a personal interest in the affairs of other people can be distorted by envy, suspicion, or any hint of prejudice against ourselves.

So it can be seen that there is a vast difference between being idly inquisitive and being truly thoughtful. The difference is temperamental, and the idle and discursive reverie of the majority is unlike the thoughtful reverie of the intelligent mind.

To most people personal contentment or discontent does not extend to any valid critical questioning of the given situation. The cat may be aware that it likes milk, but knows nothing about the manufacture of the saucer from which it drinks. The cat can also enjoy a nap on a settee without recognizing any sense of obligation to upholsterers.

Taking Everything for Granted

Some human beings accept things in much the

same way, without question. But surely a higher animal, such as a human being supposes himself to be, should be aware that you don't have to be a donkey to be an authority on hay! Is it really our function to take everything for granted with all the simplicity of a pet kitten?

Actually, quite a lot of animals show a more lively experimental and instinctive curiosity than do some people. In any period of time the majority of people have accepted prevailing conditions as being natural or inevitable, and only the most enlightened thinkers have been able to contribute something to posterity in society.

To revert to the difference again between the commonplace reverie and the creative thinking of the exceptional man, there is one basic distinction possessed by the truly intelligent, namely concentration.

CHAPTER FIVE

PREPARATION FOR MEDITATION

To be successful in any venture it is obviously necessary to pay attention to what one does. This is true of meditation practice as it is of everything else. The desire to gain self-mastery must be greater than the desire to continue existing in the old slipshod way.

Students of Hatha Yoga are well aware of this when seeking bodily self-control. It is not enough to just read books and to nod wisely at the points made with which one agrees, and then forget all about the matter. Initially at least, there must be conscious effort. Regard each new day as a goal in itself. Follow the path faithfully step by step, and soon those steps will merge as the woven pattern of a healthy and happy life.

It is worth repeating here that anyone can practise meditation with a clear conscience, for such practice is not contrary to any religious belief. Indeed, meditation is the original basis for religion, being the search for truth by the wise. An aim which is profoundly good requires no justification. Meditation can be practised by anybody, religious or non-religious.

Review Your Motives

To prepare for the practice of meditation, review your motives for wishing to follow a system of mind training. Do not work at cross purposes with yourself. Be sure that you want to succeed, and you will succeed.

See that henceforth your habits are in accordance with health promoting principles. You know what your own life is like, whether good, bad, or a mixture. Avoid dissipations and ways which are injurious to your mental and physical well-being. As far as possible, choose companions who are congenial, clean, and optimistic.

Seek out beautiful surroundings whenever you can. If you find yourself worrying, fearing, brooding, or depressed, substitute better, more positive thoughts of power, courage, success, and health.

You possess a nobler self, so allow it to find the expression it really craves. When this craving is suppressed, it is one of the causes of unhappiness and misery. Remember, the cultivation and eventual freedom of your better, truer self is your key to happiness, peace, and contentment.

Impatience is Self-defeating

These changes and improvements will not come about overnight. Do not be impatient, for impatience is self-defeating. Irritation, anger, and annoyance show a lack of power and dignity.

Preparation should be taken gently by degrees. Awareness of one's thoughts and actions is the way. Watch your reactions to life through each day. When anger or other harmful thoughts arise, remember that they are unworthy of you and do not resemble your real self. Recall that beneath your manifested weakness is that noble self that has an honourable, pleasing disposition, strong and sure.

You are capable of self-respect only if you allow your true and better nature to emerge. You probably do not waste your money, so why squander your mental energies on things of no value? If you persist in policing your mind, you will increasingly learn to avoid mental waste, and extract full value from life.

Power of Honest Reason

Since you are being asked to be self-critical to discover that which is best within yourself, it is only fair that you should be critical of this book. Do not accept anything written in it unless you can accept it with the power of honest reason.

You cannot know what meditation can do for you until you have given the practice a fair, intelligent trial. Mere credulity is one of the things one should attack within oneself. You wish to be able to think clearly, not to have your thought processes muddied by gullibility. It is only the unprejudiced, honest, and questioning mind which can arrive at truth.

The three phases of meditation, namely concentration, meditation, and contemplation, will come more easily to you if you look after your health in a sensible fashion, because the distractions caused by one complaint or another will not be there to bother you.

Each Action Depends Upon a Thought

Free investigation and true reason must guide each one upon the path to realization. Since each person is the result of his thoughts in the past, and his present thoughts will condition his future, it becomes clear that each action depends upon a thought.

Each action is only the manifestation of a thought, and so our thoughts are responsible for our actions, but we are, or should be, responsible for our thoughts. A genuine sustained and peaceful thought cannot give rise to an action of violence.

When the mind has been clarified, the light of perception shows the difference between real values and false or apparent values. Reality is easily obscured by appearances.

The meditation aspirant is setting out to gain supreme knowledge, and he must fortify his resolution by self-control over those vices which get in the way of his search. Control of the senses leads to mind control, and vice versa. Both controls should be cultivated simultaneously.

Be Aware

I once knew a Gypsy who settled temporarily in a house for personal reasons. He was fairly literate, and having a large dog, he painted the words BE AWARE OF THE DOG on his gate. Inadvertently he had given the correct wording BE AWARE instead of the more usual BEWARE.

This notice attracted some attention because of its simple novelty, and was extremely effective. In learning meditation we have to be aware to facilitate mind control, guarding against the damage of dissipating thoughts.

When the senses and the mind are calmed and controlled, we are then able to free ourselves from those prejudices which have arisen due to the habit of considering everything from a personal point of view. The obsession of separativity, the habit of constantly setting up a 'self' in opposition to 'others' prevents clear, impersonal thinking.

Clouded by Ego

To obtain true knowledge, it is absolutely essential to think impersonally, otherwise all issues are clouded by ego. In order to accomplish impersonal thinking, the student must plan out and follow a definite system of mind training, practising certain exercises to obtain concentration. When his capacity is formed for meditation, the repeated practice will create a good habit of mind.

But before attempting to practice the first step of concentration, the student should begin by training himself to observe attentively all that is going on around him. He must try to observe the phenomena of life in an *impersonal*, detached way. This is most important.

Observe as though it were some inner master self which is doing the observing, a master self which is like some visitor who is deeply interested in everything, but remains unaffected by what he sees.

This master self does in fact exist, and is the true underlying self which we are trying to promote and know. The student should also observe himself in the same way, the workings of his body and mind, his sentiments, his gestures, his motives and his thoughts.

Intelligence Destroys Ignorance

This introspection should not become morbid or sullied by conceit. The student has to study himself just as he might scrutinize the motives and actions of another person. Such attentiveness or awareness is real intelligence and should be cultivated throughout life. This systematically cultivated intelligence will sooner or later destroy ignorance.

It will be found that no longer are one's actions and thoughts spasmodic, loose, and disjointed. Worry and fear will disappear, as also will anger, and blind attachment to selfish desires.

Unrecognized selfish desires only produce worried, agitated states of mind, and these troubled states of mind must be stilled before one can meditate.

The very fact of awareness will cause one to do those things which will not only be beneficial to oneself, but also to others.

The disappearance of anger and fear will prevent one from causing harm to any living being, just as the consideration of motives will prevent any tendency to mean or dishonest actions, however small.

CHAPTER SIX

THE THREE MINDS

While practising the habits of thought in preparation for meditation, it is as well to know how the mind is constituted, so that we may have at least a working knowledge of the tools, as it were, that we are proposing to use.

It is not necessary to have a degree in psychology to understand the simple, basic facets of the mind. Anyone studying physical culture would probably become familiar with such terms as biceps, triceps, and pectoral muscles, without being a surgeon or physiotherapist. In the same way we can learn of the composition of the mind without being too recondite.

Objective, Subjective, Subconscious
First of all there is that third of the brain which is

the objective mind. If we imagine this as lying immediately behind the forehead, we have a fair enough picture of its situation.

Behind that again is the subjective mind, sandwiched between the objective and the subconscious.

Lastly, at the back of the head is the subconscious mind. Actually, the cellular nervous system is much more complicated than the three simple subdivisions I have given here, but we are not cytologists studying intricate cell structures, and so for our purposes these subdivisions are a practical working hypothesis.

The front or objective mind is that conscious mind with which we record the impressions of our waking, day to day lives. It is the ordinary thinking mind with which we see, feel, hear, and smell, and with which we decide to speak, move, or perform any other conscious action.

The subjective mind, in general terms, is where we store our recorded impressions of what we have heard, seen, felt and smelt with the objective mind. So the subjective consciousness is the realm of memory.

Mental Process of Selection

You may recall that in Chapter Two I said that we could not remember anything unless we forgot almost everything. Now is the time to qualify that statement, for what it really means is that in order to remember some fact or experience, we bring into play a mental process of selection.

It is rather like going to the larder for a particular jar of jam, and pushing aside the other jars to find the one we want at that moment. But the other jars are still there when we leave the larder.

In reality therefore, all our memories are stored for ever in the subjective mind, and if we think we have forgotten something, it is not because it has left our minds, but rather that our selective faculty is not operating as well as it might.

We have all had the slightly annoying experience of being unable to recall something when we know very well that it cannot have been 'forgotten'. We have all said, 'it's on the tip of my tongue', or, 'I just can't bring it to mind'. Later on, when the need to remember has passed, we have made the recollection.

This is because we have set up the process of selection, but our mind has been too cluttered up with other things to allow the process to work efficiently. In a later, more reflective mood, the memory has been able to come to the surface of the objective mind unhindered by other considerations of too much effort.

Subjective Storehouse

The subjective mind is not only the storehouse of those things we may sometimes wish to remember. It is the storehouse for everything, and that includes those things we feel we would like to forget. Everything is there, all the impressions, desires, passions, longings, and tendencies we have accumulated.

Those impressions and memories which we tried to cast away, the memories of which we are afraid, or find unpleasant, or feel guilty about, are all confined and repressed in the subjective storehouse. They are often the cause of nervousness, of unidentifiable and persistent anxieties, haunting fears which cloud some people's lives, and they can also be responsible for physically manifested ailments like headache, migraine, constipation and worse, all brought about by tension.

This statement is not designed to alarm you, but rather to let you see how misused thought can be, and to let you realize the power of thought for good or ill. There is no need to disown such repressions with a shudder, because that is the very reaction which made them a cause of trouble in the first place.

Freeing Repressed Thoughts

What is required is the freeing of such confined, repressed thoughts, so that they can be mastered and turned to advantage. This is not such a super-human task as it may seem, and, assuming that you are already diligently practising awareness, you are already taking steps on the path to power, wisdom, and happiness.

A psychoanalyst usually approaches problems of subjective disturbance from the objective end as it were, using a patient and sometimes tedious process in digging out the troubles.

In meditation we bring the power of the subconscious mind to bear, and you will shortly begin to see why. There is normally no need to worry about whatever repressions you may feel you have, first because worry, like envy, does not produce any practical result, and secondly because there is a safety valve which we all naturally employ.

Dreaming – the Safety Valve

Sleep is the safety valve, or, more accurately, dreaming during sleep is. When you fall asleep your objective mind rests, and your subjective mind becomes active. The watchful control of the objective is relaxed, and the result is that the subjective thoughts can express themselves in often disordered and fantastic fashion.

The non-swimmer can dream that he is swimming easily. People who are afraid of heights can dream that they are flying through the air of their own volition, and are thoroughly enjoying it.

There is no need to enlarge upon dream experiences. We all know how strange and unrelated to waking consciousness they can be. Some dreams are shocking on recollection when we remember the immoral or uncharacteristic things we have enacted in them.

In all of this there is no cause for worry once we realize that the subjective mind of sleep is a storehouse, and frequently a very jumbled storehouse at that. When our dreams or fragments of our dreams are recalled by the waking consciousness or objective mind, is there any wonder that they usually seem to be so unreasoned, foolish, impossible, or fantastic?

Symbolic Language
It must be remembered that the language of the subjective realm is symbolic. This language of symbols is largely foreign to the process of the objective consciousness.

In the course of travel I have attended many functions, weddings in India, temple services throughout the Far East, tea ceremonies in Japan, recitals of literature in Bulgaria and Rumania.

Wherever I have been, if the proceedings were conducted in a language unknown to me, then obviously although I have been able to appreciate the colour, the ritual, the physical actions and the settings, much has been lost through not understanding what was said.

It is similar with the dream state when we do not understand the meaning of the happenings, even though we may be participating in them.

What happens is that the subjective mind tries to express the things you would like to do or to have done when you were awake. It may try to enact a twenty-year-old desire which you thought was forgotten, or it may try to express something you wish you had done yesterday.

Uncontrolled Power of Fantasy

In wandering around a museum you may see objects which puzzle you because you cannot recognize the purpose for which they were made, until you read the attached explanatory description.

In your dreams your subjective mind will use symbols which you do not recognize because they are not normally associated in your rational working mind with the purposes for which they are being used in a dream. It is the uncontrolled power of fantasy and imagination.

As adults we may smile at the small boy who grips the back of the seat in front and pretends he is driving the bus, and for the moment believes that he actually is driving it. We all do things like this in our dreams, and believe in them while the dream lasts.

Actually we only ever remember a very small part of our dreams, for so much of them are deeply buried in the storehouse, and it is only those parts which lie nearest to the border of the objective that we can recall.

By now you can begin to realize what a jumbled, disorderly place the subjective consciousness can be. Knowing this, we can now move on to a consideration of the third mind, or the subconscious.

The Master Mind

The subconscious mind is the master mind, but you are not normally aware of its existence. From the moment of your conception it has worked unceasingly to build you, sustain, and repair you. It communicates with every organ and part of your body through a complicated system of nerve cells. It regulates your very existence by its nervous energy, controlling your heart beats, as well as the functioning of everything else within the body.

We take for granted the action of liver, bowels, digestive organs, and so forth. But without the control of the subconscious mind over every bodily function, we may imagine what would happen.

When we move to avoid colliding with something, or raise an arm to drive off a fly, we are conscious of the action involved, and we are also dimly conscious of some thought which preceded the action. When the subconscious mind works, which it does all the time, we are not conscious of thought.

We do not think about our heart beats unless they are disturbed, any more than we think about our digestive processes unless they give us discomfort. Yet both objective and subconscious thought exists, but are different in that one is conscious of the first and not the second.

They are also different because the objective mind is limited by the ability of its owner to think, whereas the subconscious mind is limited only by the demands made upon it. Given a job to do, the subconscious mind will do it but first it must be asked, if the task is different from those it is used to doing automatically.

Getting the Subconscious to Work for Us

Having discovered now the power of the subconscious mind, the next question is how to send to it those thoughts which we wish to realize, or in other words, how we can get our subconscious minds working for us under direct control.

It is a fact that your health, your wisdom, your success or your failure, all depend upon the way in which your subconscious mind is working.

We probably all know of someone who rarely becomes ill, if ever, and who is cheerful, courageous and confident. That person is one who is blessed with an ability to draw upon his subconscious mind in a positive way. Such a person may not necessarily realize how they are doing it, but doing it they are.

Mere attempts at 'auto-suggestion' can be dangerous in the following way. You may have met someone who tells you that if they have a headache for example, they just 'think it away', or repeatedly tell themselves that the headache is getting better and it goes away. A few people can do this sort of thing successfully, but most cannot.

Concentration

The danger lies in possible lack of concentration. If this method is attempted, it frequently happens that either the objective mind begins as it were to dispute the desire, and the headache then becomes worse, or the mind is so easily distracted by other thoughts or desires that nothing is accomplished and the headache goes on.

Such mistakes are most unfortunate. If the conscious mind begins to doubt and to argue with its own assertions, the doubt usually takes over the desire and reverses it. This frequently happens too when the mind is easily distracted from its purpose.

So what is required is our old friend, concentration. You will remember that at the beginning of this section I described the three minds as being situated with the objective in front, the subjective in the middle, and the subconscious at the back.

Since the objective mind is the one which can knowingly formulate a thought, it has to get that thought through the subjective to the subconscious, for the subconscious to get working on it. Only then can the thought be acted upon in a positive way for it to be definitely brought to fruition.

But we have already seen that the middle or subjective mind seizes upon conscious thoughts and stores them away, to produce them again either as memories or as parts of dream symbolism. The problem then, is how to get thoughts through the subjective without them being lost, stolen, or otherwise delayed.

Isolating a Particular Thought

There is only one way in which this can be done, and that is by isolating a particular thought. Only the single, undeviating thought can get through. And since, as we have seen, thoughts follow each other in rapid succession, the next difficulty is how to isolate one thought by arresting this rapid, continuous flow.

It is now evident that mind control is necessary for the purpose, the mind training for such control being meditation, beginning with the first stage, concentration.

CHAPTER SEVEN

THE SEARCH

Assuming that you have been practising the suggestions given in Chapter Five, you will already have begun to heighten your powers of concentration and perception. Your self-awareness diligently pursued will have modified your emotions and brought them under control.

Some people, missing the point of 'self-awareness' and mistaking it to mean a mere preoccupation with egotism, have thought such practice to be selfish. Certainly it would be so if devoted to the ego. But detached observation of one's own being is neither selfish nor unselfish, for the aim is ego-lessness. It is in fact all we can do.

If we regard society as sick, we shall not heal it by being passively infected by it, but living our own well-balanced lives as best we can, in spite of it.

The positive thinking man avoids the flabby attitude of the drifter who constantly moans, 'why doesn't somebody do something?' He also avoids the other extreme of the man who has the panacea for all ills, which usually means a compulsive expression of personal prejudices.

The reasoning man attempts to put his own inner house in order first, because he is honest enough to acknowledge that he has to some degree helped to create the society in which he lives. In dealing successfully with his own problems and personality, he thereby helps others in the best way he can.

True Refuge Within Yourself

To fly to external refuges is only to be ultimately disappointed. Your true refuge is within yourself, and your own created attitude colours your own personal world. Most of the woes known to man spring from ignorance of the fact that there is something behind the mind.

The apparent constant agitations of life are there for the person who does not know what 'Is'. We project our inward pattern upon outward circumstances. If the inward pattern is frequently faulty, then our outward circumstances will frequently seem faulty too. Ignorant men blame the circumstances for the shortcomings. Wise men look within.

A mind caught up in contradictions jumps about like a scalded animal, and tries to grasp at too many alternatives to ever know peace. A mind agitated about its shortcomings is bad. A mind agitated about its agitations is worse. A mind that meditates knows that what 'Is' is much more important than what ought to be. When you know what 'Is', you can make it a starting point for a new and better life.

The Ancient Wisdom

Let the ancient wisdom, that is also in you, look down calmly, tolerantly, compassionately on the foolish mind of today, not interfering agitatedly, only observing and wondering, and then in the mad rush of life the mind of wisdom will remember the calmer heights of being, and you will relax.

From exactly the same roots of human folly, bad habits, and cramped narrowness, some people follow what seems like an inevitable course of distorted life, while others achieve serenity and inward strength. Obviously then, there does exist a quality which enables a man to shake off his poisonous habits.

Accessible to All

Fortunately this quality is accessible to all. It does not require a magnificent intelligence quotient or a degree pass in some subject. This quality may be recognized in anyone, because it is common to all.

The only requirement necessary to discovering it is to realize that it is within you, and can therefore be found by diligent searching. So if such a quality is accessible, only the deliberate neglect of it can lead to moral evil.

Ignorance is the basic fault. The word ignorance has an unpleasant sound, and may make us think of a filthy slum, or a bare, cold room.

Unfortunately, many people dwell in the mental ignorance of a kind of lazy pipe dream, imagining to themselves all the nice things they would like to be, and running away from anything they think might spoil the pipe dream.

Life versus Dreams

Of course one of the things that is always trying to spoil the pipe dream is life itself, attempting to carry the stagnant dream thoughts into a clear stream of existence.

Many people lie and fight and cheat like mad to remain in the seemingly cosy fug of ignorance, like some dissipated clubman who believes his only happiness is in a smoke-filled atmosphere.

Yet it is possible to know ourselves, to know our motives (bad or good as they may be), our powers and limitations, our past follies and wrongs, and with this knowledge comes detachment. Waking from the dream is deliverance and freedom.

Instead of taking the stage obsessed by the great tragedy of the little ego and being fit only for crowd scenes, we can become aware of the entire tragicomedy of humanity and can then act accordingly.

CHAPTER EIGHT

THE PRACTICE

We have all heard of the sixth sense, have heard such sayings as; 'Some sixth sense warned me', or 'some sixth sense told me that ...'. The mundane senses are five, namely: smell, hearing, touch, taste, and sight. The sixth sense is the mind, but it is the mind sharpened, wise, accomplished, polished as the ancient Chinese used to say, 'to face-seeing keenness'.

State of Detachment

Before this can be achieved the student must be ready to embark upon his first experience of meditation by being in a state of detachment which has cleared his thoughts of the negative defilements.

You cannot see a jewel dropped in a muddy pool.

The mind must be cleared of selfish aims, of hatred, envy, greed, and desire. You wish to start on a new, pure journey, unmitigated by the accretions of the old way of life, therefore the canvas must be blank, the paint fresh.

Having practised the preparation for meditation as previously described, you should be already well on the way to acquire detachment.

The method of meditation given here is one of many methods, and another method will be given. They are suitable for anyone, but particularly for Westerners, differing only in minor details which allow for personal choice.

It should be understood that although based on the breaths, these methods are not 'breathing exercises'. The object here is not chest expansion or physical vigour, neither are these meditations similar to the breathing 'gymnastics' of the Hindu yoga systems.

Supernormal Faculties

Results such as supernormal faculties and the production of phenomena can be gained or experienced in time through the practices given in this book, but you are warned that exciting or attractive as this may sound, they are *always* to be regarded as incidental trifles, mere interesting gifts on the way, not to be unduly prized.

For if you should experience supernormal manifestations and seize upon them, your practice will go no further, and you will not achieve the ultimate aim of real freedom and control.

If you proceed knowing that such phenomena are incidental and trifling, you will go on to discover much more of far greater value. And by proceeding you will eventually be able to relegate such things to a proper mundane perspective, realizing that they are property common to wisdom and inner perception.

'Watch the Breaths'

The practices given here forbid any sort of abnormal breathing. Indeed the normal breathing is not in any way to be forced or voluntarily suspended. The student is only required to 'watch the breaths', and, noting their variations closely, to attain true concentration. The process is recommended to both the 'dulled' and the imaginative temperament alike.

By 'dulled' here is meant the mind that has tended to become unable to appreciate the working of cause and effect in the moral plane. The mind awakened by meditation is capable of much more than average intelligence.

No meditation can be practised successfully without some measure of intelligence and penetration. In other words, without some power of concentration there can be no wisdom, and without a modicum of wisdom there can be no concentration. This leaves the field open to practically everyone.

It will be found by the beginner that the object of concentration is inconstant and evanescent. As one gradually advances, the more difficult it seems to become for a while, for respiration becomes fine almost to vanishing point, and the 'object' of meditation is thus 'lost', to the bewilderment of the inexperienced tiro. This is quite natural at first to those unused to even a slightly extended period of concentration.

Position for this Meditation

If you are able to take up the complete 'lotus' position of sitting on the floor with the left foot crossed on to the right thigh, and the right foot on left thigh, then by all means do so. This was the position favoured by the ancients. Being used to it, they found it comfortable; the back was maintained erect, and breathing unimpaired.

This is also the position favoured by the modern masters, and it is well worth while attempting it for a few minutes every day until you can use it. But do not force it, let it come gradually, and eventually you can become supple enough to adopt it for purposes of meditation.

For those who cannot sit in the lotus position, sitting down on the floor cross-legged will do. Whatever position one adopts, it must fulfil three conditions: comfort, a straight back, and easy breathing. Lying down is unsuitable as it induces drowsiness. Standing and walking are no good as they bias towards restlessness.

Places Suitable for Meditation

If you are fortunate enough in good weather to find a secluded outdoor spot where you can be undisturbed, it will be suitable for meditation. Probably most people will find a quiet room the best place. In the beginning loud or harsh noise is inimical to meditation, so do find the quietest place you possibly can. Make sure that you will not be disturbed by anyone.

Meditate alone, unless you are fortunate enough to share your practice with a qualified master, which in most cases is unlikely. Do not ask your close friends or relations to join you, for, however sympathetic they may be, their presence will disturb your concentration, because you will think of them and become embarrassed.

How to Begin

Allowing for at least an hour-and-a-half to elapse after a meal, have a good wash or a bath, dress in loose, comfortable clean clothes, and take up your meditation position. If it is more comfortable for you, place a couple of cushions alongside each other to sit on. Do not lean your back against a chair or wall or anything.

Having sat down, ignore all the distracting thoughts of business, relatives, disease, worry, and doubt. Do not fight such thoughts, but as they arise, gently as it were, look at them as though they did not belong to you or concern you. If you fight them violently back, they will only intensify and take away your concentration.

Rays of Good Will

Instead of giving consideration to them, mentally project a thought of well-wishing towards all living beings in front of you, to infinity. This thought must not be directed at any particular individual, but must be all-encompassing, as if rays of good will were emanating to all beings ahead of you. On no account must the rays be visualized as returning to oneself.

When you are satisfied that the thought has projected without any feeling of self-interest, the same procedure should be enacted to the right side, without turning the head. Then, still looking ahead, the thought should be projected to the back, then to the left. Next, beneath one, and lastly, above.

This preliminary helps to purify the mind, driving out feelings of selfishness, enmity, and pettiness, where they exist. The fact of not directing the thought towards any favoured individual disallows any possibility of motivation creeping in. So does the idea of not desiring the thought to come back to oneself.

Remember, you are detached, freed from usual involvements. You have now put aside pride and self-delusion, and your mind is compassionate, calm, trustful and devoted, allowing you to reflect upon the incomparable virtues of the mind behind the mind, or if you like, the true self.

Stage 1: Counting the Breaths

Sitting cross-legged, or in the half lotus or full lotus position, with right hand resting flat on the palm of the left hand, with the ends of the two thumbs touching, lightly close the eyes and, keeping the back straight, start breathing gently to a mental count of *FIVE*.

Breathe in slowly to *ONE*, breathe out to *TWO*, in to *THREE*, and so on. After the *FIFTH* breath, begin again at *ONE*, and repeat the process.

Actually, you can choose any number to breathe to between five and ten. But do decide on a specific terminal number and then stick to it. If a definite number is not adhered to, it can be distracting, because some people start asking inner questions about which is the 'best' number, and even become doubtful or superstitious about it.

A count of less than five is too short and therefore disturbing, while a count of more than ten diverts attention from breaths to counts and breaks the concentration that way.

Make the count at the end of the breath and this will help to establish a precise rhythm at first. This is also to prevent the mind following the breaths internally and possible speculation on physiological process.

What you should do is fix the attention on the breaths going in and out of the nostrils, concentrating on the point just under the nose where the breath enters and leaves.

Rhythm of the Count

Just as the breath should not be followed internally, neither should it be followed externally. Pay no attention to what happens 'outside'. Simply watch mentally the breaths going in and out of the nostrils to the rhythm of the count.

The purpose of this part of the practice is to gain concentration which will lead on to full meditation. Practise at least once a day when you can be alone and undisturbed.

The duration of each session is a personal matter. You will find, when the practice becomes a habit that you will tend to establish a regular period because your power of concentration has strengthened with use.

The question of how long one should continue with this first stage practice of counting breaths depends upon how soon one is able to focus the concentration upon the breaths alone, without counting. This will vary with different people, according to how well developed were the powers of concentration before practice was first begun.

However, gentle perseverence will win the day, and there is no need for impatience, worry, or feelings of frustration.

When, after a few days or weeks of regular practice you can dispense with the counting, being able to concentrate on the breaths alone, then you are ready to commence the next stage.

Stage 2: Following the Breath

When one can successfully dispense with counting, the second stage is reached. Although at this point it is possible for the student to practise the breathing without counting, it will be found that the mind will tend to wander. Instead of counting, one must now mentally 'follow the breath' down inside to a spot just below the rib-cage, the solar plexus, and back out again, repeating the process over and over.

The concentration is now to be upon the area

followed by each breath, that is from the nostrils through the chest and down to the solar plexus, then back again. These are the limits and they should not be exceeded.

Some people feel unsure as to where exactly the solar plexus lies, but there is no need for concern about this. If you do not follow the breaths below the point where the two lower ribs spread from the centre of the body, or even to the navel, you will not exceed the necessary area of concentration.

As with the first stage, this second stage is to be practised until perfect, that is to say, until the observation of the breaths has become automatic.

Stage 3: Concentration on Breath Contact

The purpose of the practice of the second stage was to establish an automatic 'consciousness' of the breaths going in at the nostrils and down to the midriff, then back again. When this process is firmly established, the third stage can begin.

Now is the time to place the attention on the breath entering and leaving the nostrils. This is done without the necessity of counting, and without the necessity of following the breath.

The previous two stages have eliminated those necessities, and the student will, having persevered, be able to concentrate on the breath in an automatic rhythm given by the first stage, just as he will have gained an automatic consciousness of the whole swing of each breath from nostrils to solar plexus without having to think about it.

A simile may be useful here. It is as if one were a watchman at a city gate who examines those entering or departing, but who does not worry or concern himself about those inside or outside. This simile of 'watching at the gate' can well be applied to the breaths entering and leaving the 'nose-door'.

This form of concentration will allay the wasteful

passions and obsessive thought conceptions, clearing the mind in readiness for the fourth stage of practice.

Breathing Becomes Refined

The 'profit' yet to be gained is the destruction of the fetters of the mind to leave it pure, wholesome, and under full control. The great difference between this form of meditation practice, and other practices in which some material object is used, is that whereas an object becomes more vivid, here we find that breathing apparently tends to fade. Actually it does not really fade, but becomes refined and is not noticed because of the intense concentration and absorption being increasingly gained.

There is absolutely no need for concern, you will not 'stop' breathing, and in any case the point made should be superfluous, since if the practice has been faithful you will already be well on the way beyond negative 'worry'.

Up to now consciousness of, and concentration upon, the breathing has been the 'object' used for this meditation. But because the student has trained his body and mind into a state of purity by faithfully following the practice in all of its aspects, he now slides gently into finer and finer breathing of which he is still aware, till at last he slips into a state where he is at a loss to find that breathing has become imperceptible.

This occurs very gradually, in rather the same way as the decreasing reverberations of a bell sound after the last stroke upon the bell.

When Breathing Becomes Imperceptible

When the 'object' or sign of breathing has disappeared, one does not relinquish the practice. Full absorption has not yet been gained. What should be done at the time when breathing becomes imperceptible, is to ponder gently upon the fact by mentally considering these three questions: 'Who is it who is *not* breathing?' 'Who is it who *is* breathing?' 'Where is the breathing?'

In the state of high concentration thus reached, the student is able to put these questions in a quite detached way, and is gaining ground in the practice of neighbourhood concentration, or if you like, partial absorption.

One can now realize that the thought of inspiration was one thought, the thought of expiration another, and of the point of entry and exit of the breath yet another thought. The help of all three thoughts was necessary during the stages of training, to enable the student to reach the state of neighbourhood concentration or partial absorption.

But it will also be realized that *three* thoughts do not tend to concentration, and so it was necessary to learn how to merge the three thoughts into one. So when breathing has apparently ceased, it is a sign that one thought is being achieved instead of three.

The 'Nose-door'

The next step is to reinstate or recommence meditation upon the point where the breath strikes on entering and leaving, namely the 'nose-door'. By now one has acquired sufficient concentration to do this.

Fix the attention upon where the breath enters and leaves the nostrils. It should not be necessary to remind the student that he is detached, and that therefore he does not merely think of a 'nose' or physical attributes. He simply concentrates upon that area at which the breath comes in and out, this now being the 'object' to the exclusion of all else.

With concentration for rein, and penetration for

goad, the student resolutely gets his purpose out of the apparently missing breaths.

This condition of seemingly suspended breaths is equivalent to the acquired 'sign' or 'object' of other forms of meditation.

The student is now still at a stage of preliminary concentration, though he has risen above his 'original sign' of the breaths. Soon, before many days have passed, the 'reflex image' is also attained. This attainment begins the next and fourth stage.

Stage 4: Placing the Mind on the State of Absorption

The reflex image with the gain of which begins the fourth stage, has not the same appearance to everyone. The phenomena comes to some with a sense of great comfort, ease of silky softness, or as sweet and pleasant gentle winds. Others have compared the phenomena to the shining of stars, a beautiful round jewel, a silvery chain, a garland of flowers, a column of smoke, a magnificent cloud, a brilliant wheel, a full moon, a sun, and so on.

The aspect of the phenomena depends entirely on the ideas and cognizing powers of the student, for it is the cognizing faculty that gives rise to these various semblances taken by the reflex image. Therefore it would be no help to a student to suggest what might occur, as this could give rise to the suggestion being adopted and this would be false. The student should *always* discover his own reflex image for himself.

A true teacher of meditation never tells a student what to expect as a reflex image, thus obviating the charge that he may have placed it in the student's mind.

What the Teacher Should Say

Another point arising here is what the teacher

should say to the student who says that he has gained a reflex image. There are two schools of thought; one holds that the teacher should not say, 'Yes, you have now gained a reflex image', because the student might become too satisfied and subsequently relax his efforts, and eventually lose all he had gained.

On the other hand, if the teacher says the attainment is not enough and the student must strive on, there is the danger that the student, full of joy with his new discovery, will be discouraged and lose heart, and in that way relax his exertions.

In fact, both of the above replies to the student can be correct when given to different individuals by a truly accomplished meditation master: because the teacher would reply in accordance with his understanding of the temperaments of his pupils.

I have raised this point on the assumption that readers do not have recourse to a personal teacher. The thing to do in meditation practice is to always carry on, whatever the attainment reached. In any case, the time comes when the practice becomes a part of existence which the student will never relinquish.

Controlled Mind

Having gained the reflex image, this image is now the 'object' of concentration. At this stage the student will find during meditation that the hindrances of mundane cravings are suppressed, and that the mind is calm and powerful, free of discursiveness, and controlled.

The reflex image must be protected by the student. He must not reflect on colour, shape, or transience of the 'object', but must simply hold the image with the calm detachment of his training. He is to keep it before his mind's eye, but is not to go into the minutiae of it, for that would destroy the concentration.

Ultimately will arise the power to put aside all obstacles and worldly cares, and to this end the reflex image must be fostered and advanced. It must be made to grow at will until it seems to fill all space. This brings the tiro to a state of complete absorption.

Five Special Accomplishments

When complete absorption has been assiduously cultivated for some time, five special accomplishments are gained. They are; power of instant reflection; power of instant attainment; power of instant emergence from an attainment; power of making things come to pass by sheer will force; power of contemplation for reviewing and investigation.

After the meditation is perfected, one no longer needs to begin again at the counting stage and go through all the stages to attain absorption. Perfected, the meditation is acquired for life, and one can then go about one's daily affairs having the ability to slip into full absorption whenever desired.

Only, and this is absolutely essential, one's purity of virtue must be maintained intact; there must be *no* killing, dishonesty, lusting, falsehood, addiction to intoxicants, cruelty, harshness, anger or envy, on the part of one who wishes to preserve his powers unimpaired. This is the only way to safeguard the faculty for absorption.

At this stage the meditation or absorption can be prolonged as much as desired. There are masters who have remained in meditation for as long as seven days and longer, though these are special cases for special purposes and there is no profitable use in such excessive periods for most people, even if they were practicable, which, in the case of the layman, they are not.

What is to be remembered is that the mental forces should be maintained in perfect equality. The mental forces are confidence, energy, mindfulness or awareness, concentration, and wisdom. These must be well balanced.

Once or twice a day in meditation is enough, and the accomplished student will gradually transcend the initial absorption factors of sustained application, joy, and happiness, until, retaining only perfectly focused thought and equanimity, he gains still higher absorptions that lead to the hypercosmic regions of being.

The Path of Insight

Now the explanation of the first four stages of this meditation is complete up to the attainment of absorption. This absorption, in the highest sense, is still only mundane, although it is yet supernormal. With the means to switch on this keen 'absorption-mind', is also the ability to penetrate the nature of things as they really are, and one can select meditations to this end.

They may be meditations on suffering or transience, and suddenly in a moment of insight the student gains his first glimpse into the ultramundane, and knowledge of himself as one who has entered a hitherto quite unknown state.

Then gone forever are false views and doubts. Something never before imagined in the individual life has been actually experienced. This insight, this revelation of changeless peace, is the ultimate aim of the meditator.

Even in dreams there can sometimes occur occasional flashes of what is, in waking life, called 'reality', or what is considered useful or of intellectual moment. This does not prove that dream life as a whole, is real. Yet neither does the solid-seeming waking life deserve the name 'real', if judged from the viewpoint of meditation, although what might be called flashes of value for the appreciation and realization of that viewpoint can and do occur in both dream and waking life.

Intuitive Flashes

Which means that despite the fact that the person, or instrument, is unreal in both dream and waking life, intuitive flashes can illuminate each of them, though they are flashes which are not *of* them. Such intuitions occur to everyone in greater or lesser degree, and their internal development will cause these 'flowers of thought' to grow.

When dreams occur, however grotesque, they seem real enough while they are being experienced, and are recollected as fantastic when the dreamer awakes. When the great awakening of meditation occurs, then the seeming reality about us is also brought into true perspective, and we see existence as it really is.

Even now, through the discoveries of science, we can reject much of ostensible form, sensation, perception, experience, and consciousness itself, which would once have been regarded as witness of actuality. A glance through a microscope or a telescope can show us much of which we were unaware.

The intense illumination of penetrant insight dissipates the whole illusion. So the practised meditator wisely realizes the transitory nature of all phenomena, even the highest, and determines to attain the Permanent.

CHAPTER NINE

SOME QUESTIONS ANSWERED

For those who have read so far but who have not yet begun to practise meditation, this might be a useful place in the book to answer questions which may have arisen in their minds.

How Long for Practice?

Some people have asked how long a period they should set aside for the practice, and at what time of day. There are no hard and fast rules on this and it will depend on personal inclination. Fifteen to thirty minutes a day is usually sufficient for a beginner, but as the practice strengthens there will be a tendency to prolong the exercise according to the greater power of concentration gradually being achieved.

The time of day for practice is again a matter of preference, though having established a set time it is best to stick to it, as the body and mind then become attuned to a regular habit of concentration. When one becomes quite adept, it is then easy to practice whenever desired.

Meditation should never be hurried. To establish an initial pattern, all that is necessary is to note the time of commencement. It does not matter how long the practice lasts, so long as it is sincere.

So do not be concerned with the time of finishing, for you cannot meditate and watch the clock at the same time. You will automatically realize when you are quite unable to sustain the practice any longer. One should however, persevere, and not just give in to laziness.

If you practise in the morning it gives serenity to the rest of the day. If you practise before going to bed, it gives serenity to sleep. Try to ensure that there is nothing in the room which might seriously affect one's early attempts.

Photographs with personal connotations are an example of objects which may be disturbing to the beginner. On the other hand, a relaxed atmosphere conducive to meditation may be assisted by pleasant paintings on the walls of the room.

Positions for Meditation

In Chapter Eight I mentioned positions which may be adopted for meditation. If you really cannot use a cross-legged position, then sit in a straight-backed chair with the hands resting along each knee. This position is the one favoured by the ancient Egyptian priests and god-kings, and is familiar to most people through pictures of old statues.

Whatever the posture used, the spine and head should be erect and the body held perfectly still, not tensed, but naturally braced. The fitter the body is, the easier the practice will be.

It is a good idea to accustom oneself regularly to the chosen position before attempting meditation, for the purpose is to be able to meditate without the body intruding upon the concentration. Meditation cannot be performed, especially in the early stages, if there is discomfort.

Is Meditation Hypnosis?

I have been asked if meditation is a form of hypnosis. Meditation is not hypnosis, but is sense-withdrawal of a most highly concentrated kind. Actually, such sense-withdrawal or sense-detachment is practised by all of us in our daily lives to some extent.

To get things done in life we all develop concentration to a degree. People say they become accustomed to the regular ticking of a clock for example, and do not notice it. Yet when the clock stops, they become aware of the fact. This is because the mind has become used to the ticking sound, has unconsciously accepted it, and detached the objective consciousness from it. When the sound stops there arises a conscious reaction to the difference.

Being bombarded by a multiplicity of sense impressions, we have to be selective and choose those we wish to utilize for a present and particular purpose. How successful we may be with our selection depends upon the degree of concentration we possess.

In meditation the entire external world is shut out because the meditator has the ability to check the outgoing powers of the mind and direct them inwards. It is integration of the previously dissipated mental energies. This control of the senses has nothing to do with hypnotism.

Whole Mind Working in Unity

The state of mind in meditation is exactly the opposite of hypnosis. In hypnotism, part of the mind is lulled to sleep, leaving another part free to work. Sometimes, especially in the case of a mind that is fighting against itself, this makes the free part of the mind stronger, and in the absence of opposition, better able to do its work.

Indeed the part of the mind, since it is not fighting against itself, can do exceedingly more than the whole mind if that whole mind is disunited. Nevertheless, there is still only a portion of the mind at work when a person is hypnotized.

On the other hand, in meditation, the whole mind is awake, alert, alive and working in unity, once it has gained the mastery given by the practice.

Physical Sensations During Meditation

It may be that questions will arise in the mind of the

student who experiences certain physical sensations during meditation. Sometimes there is felt a kind of mild 'pins and needles' sensation. A student may find that his body seems to sway slightly from side to side. Then too, some find themselves falling very slowly backwards.

If any of these sensations, or others, are experienced, there is no cause for alarm. Such sensations are never unpleasant, and are not harmful. They are not to be looked for, and should be given no importance if they arise. Really, they are merely signs of unaccustomed relaxation, and in some cases point to the fact that increased concentration is being achieved.

If the sensations interfere greatly with the meditation, then the student must decide for himself whether or not to cease practising for the time being, and rest. His decision will depend upon how tired he may feel.

If the student does stop meditating for the moment, he may be sure that he will look forward with pleasant anticipation to his next attempt. These physical sensations very quickly cease altogether if practice is regular.

A 'Trance' State

Finally, I have often been asked by fearful people if there is a possibility that one may not return from a 'trance' state. This supposition is quite unfounded. My usual answer has been that the difficulty is never in 'coming back' but rather in getting there, and when there, in staying there!

In the first place, meditation is quite natural and is not a cataleptic trance, there is no loss of consciousness or muscular rigidity or other phenomena connected with certain forms of illness, and, as has already been pointed out, the mind is fully under control all the time during practice.

CHAPTER TEN

THE MEDITATION OF COMPASSION

There are people who question 'faith' as an article of belief, and who even reject religious teaching if the emphasis is placed upon 'praying to believe'. Such people see no logical use in being asked to accept a 'blind belief'. Since they cannot have 'faith' in what they consider 'blind belief', they have at least the honesty to admit their feeling, if only to themselves.

Possibly the word faith might be translated as 'confidence'. It is rather hard to translate as it connotes a certain degree of enthusiasm as being a part of it. It is more the confidence one might have in a doctor who has cured you, and to whom you would eagerly go again if you became ill, for you would have 'faith' in him.

To really understand the 'Why' of life one needs a degree of experience, a little intuition and the sort of faith already mentioned, plus intelligence and energy all combined, in order to begin to understand. Then one must develop all of these to gain insight, which is really a fusion of the qualities named.

Individual Personality

At this point it is necessary to explain briefly the idea of the individual personality in order to explain more fully the process of meditation. But please do not believe what I say out of 'blind faith'. You would be wrong to force belief or to suspend disbelief.

All I ask of the reader here is to take as a theory something which has been understood and therefore believed in by great men down through the ages. So there may be, for you, 'something in it'.

The practice of the development of insight can, and if properly done and persisted in will, clear the whole screen of the mind.

The mind has been likened to a fishing net with a lot of little knots. 'Information', for instance, runs through these, and since all are joined, the clearing of a mind blockage clears a lot of channels and obviously makes for a clearer mind.

Body-Mind-Spirit Complex

Now although we usually think of 'my body', 'my will', and 'my thought' as almost separate entities, and rightly so in most contexts, in reality we are a body-mind-spirit complex, indivisible.

After that preliminary, how does one evaluate onself? How does one really find the 'Why' of life?

The answer for both questions is in the same way and on the same path. And the path followed is the same one for all people, whether it is done in the name of a particular religion or not.

Some people do not travel the path at all, some turn and go the other way, some go off on a side path, some go slowly, some go relatively quickly, some stop and play games; but to know, to attain real knowledge, one must travel this path.

And the path is so clear, so simple, but difficult to follow. Its very simplicity deludes, because people look for something complex in such matters. There are those who can help, by pointing out the way; but nobody, not even the greatest, can take you along. You yourself must make the effort.

The Development of Tranquillity

So, and some of this is bound to be reiteration, here is the way. It is in two parts. The first is the development of tranquillity.

Sit very comfortably, alert but not tense,

observing only one real pre-requisite, that the spine must be kept as straight as possible.

Breathe deeply, slowly, regularly, rhythmically, letting the breath come down to the pit of the stomach. For some people this requires practice.

Then summon up mindfulness, attention, and think of loving-kindness, concentrating upon it, not thinking *ABOUT* it but concentrating on it, until you can quite wordlessly be aware of that mainly. (Later one endeavours to be aware of that to the exclusion of everything else, but that comes with practice.)

Then mentally beam out this loving-kindness like a searchlight or a lighthouse to all living, sentient beings in front of one, right to the uttermost bounds of space and beyond, then swing your mental beam to the right, then behind, then to the left, then downwards, then upwards, *TO ALL EQUALLY*.

Impartial Loving-Kindness

The feeling of loving-kindness must be absolutely impartial, and it is important that thoughts of friends, loved ones, those you admire, those who have done you a good turn, are not dwelt upon. And likewise thoughts of those who are the opposite to these things should not be dwelt upon either. Loving-kindness should go to all equally.

Then the method is repeated again, but this time the thought is that which is often translated as 'Compassion', being a sort of desire to protect others, all equally, and the practice is carried out as above.

After this, one switches to 'Joy in the gains and attainments of others', again using the same method.

Here it should be explained that 'loving-kindness' is active loving-kindness. 'Compassion' is preventive loving-kindness, that is, a desire to ward off sorrow from all equally. 'Joy in the gains and attainments of others' is disinterested loving-kindness, that is, loving-kindness devoid of all self-interest.

Finally one switches to complete disinterestedness in the sense of complete tranquillity, in which no separateness, and no 'oneness' for that matter, exists.

By switching, it might be more correct to understand that one feeling grows out of the other rather than a sudden switching. The practices described above help all beings as well as oneself, and personal concentration and tranquillity is gained.

The Development of Insight

It is wise not to attempt the development of insight without first having gained tranquillity. It is well to remember that love without power can bring happiness; both together can bring happiness and emancipation. Power without love can only bring tragedy.

For the development of insight, one sits in the same position as for other practices. It is possible to concentrate the attention on one of several things. Here I shall give only two as these are best for all types of person, and are the two upon which the mystics lay great stress. They may be done alternately, or only one may be chosen. It does not matter.

The first method is to concentrate on the breath, being aware of it as it is inhaled and exhaled, knowing when one is breathing in a short breath, or breathing in and out long or short breaths. This is done wordlessly and dispassionately. I will repeat this, as it is most important. One does this wordlessly and dispassionately *AND WITHOUT THINKING* either of other things or of what one is doing, being just a dispassionate observer.

Naturally thoughts will arise at first, in this as in preceding practices. One does not try to 'shoo' them away and one does not dwell on them, and one is not sorry or perturbed at their arising.

Concentration on Feeling

In the second method, instead of concentrating on the breath, one concentrates on feeling, either physical or mental, as it arises and passes away in the body or the mind. This is done in just the same way as concentration on breathing, wordlessly, dispassionately, as a mere observer of the phenomena.

When concentration has been gained by either or both of these methods, it is then possible to turn the light of that concentration on to thoughts, noticing how they too arise and pass away. It is seen that this arising and passing away goes on all the time, ceaselessly, until eventually 'thought' stops. Then one is enabled to see what it is that transcends thought.

When this is achieved the 'slate of mind' is wiped clean, giving power and loving-kindness.

Even after such achievement, the result may not necessarily be noticed or appreciated by the crowd, but by that time one has transcended the idea of 'what do they think of me' among many other such ideas.

The achievement brings happiness, peace, tranquillity, and equanimity.

CHAPTER ELEVEN

LIFE FROM A MEDITATION POINT OF VIEW

In everyday life we are faced with a succession of problems. These are generally minor problems, but occasionally there arises a major problem involving an emotional crisis, and creating deep-seated disruptions.

Most of our problems concern practical matters rather than theoretical or philosophical ones. We may have domestic responsibilities that are too heavy for us, or we are short of money, or the neighbours are noisy. Since these sort of problems are apparently practical ones, an approach to them by way of any kind of philosophy would seem at first to have no value.

The practice of meditation uncovers suffering, its origin, and the way leading to its cure. Again, superficially, this would seem to have only a distant relationship to our immediate and everyday problems.

Certainly meditation will not give us an instantaneous solution to our problems. It takes time and practice, and is not a miracle-working formula which will solve everything in a day. In contending with our domestic responsibilities, or our lack of money, or in wondering what to do about our noisy neighbours, teachings about tranquillity, insight, and enlightenment all seem very remote.

Yet what we have to remember is that the various practical problems are the occasions of suffering or disturbance, not their origins. Although we must try to deal with the manifestations, it is a bit like getting rid of the spots without curing the measles.

There is no short-term solution to the

fundamental problems of life. It is possible to obscure the symptoms of a disease, while its real cause remains untouched.

Meditation Attacks Problems at Roots

The meditation way then, can only solve our problems by attacking them at their origins, not at their surface manifestations. Indeed, they can be finally solved in no other way. The origin or root cause of all problems is ignorance. The ignorance may be simply that of not understanding the cause. It can be the primal blindness that prevents us from discerning the true nature of existence.

This ignorance makes us seek a permanent personal happiness (often of a material order) in an unsatisfactory world of impermanence and illusion.

The basic ignorance manifests as delusion about the true nature of things, as greed in all its forms, mild or intense, and as hatred, as well as aversion of various kinds.

From these roots of delusion, greed, and hate, all of the unwholesome mind factors are derived. These in turn create wrong will-activity, which builds up reactions leading to unhappiness or suffering.

Nature of Mind Factors Involved

That which makes will-activity right or wrong, good or bad, wholesome or unwholesome, is itself the nature of the mind factors involved. Any will-activity which has its roots in delusion, greed, or hate is morally wrong and will bring about future suffering. Any will-activity which springs from the opposites, discernment, generosity, and goodwill, is bound to bring about happiness in the future and to make for progress as morally good, or skilful thinking.

Wrong will-activity is primarily the arising of unwholesome mind factors, and because of the retarding and damaging effects of these adverse determinants, efforts towards better development should first of all be directed towards preventing them from arising. To do this completely takes a great deal of self-discipline, a strong and continual exertion of will-power. This is the first great effort, the first aspect of self-control to be considered.

Self-control Begins with Awareness

In this effort, it is necessary to become fully aware of the ways in which wrong or harmful thoughts arise, the ways in which they bring about wrong speech and the ways in which they bring about unskilful activity. Self-control must begin with awareness.

Self-control done in this way cannot lead to repression, since repression is a matter of forcing ideas below the level which is normally accessible to consciousness, whereas self-control by awareness is a rational process of keeping ideas within the full scope of consciousness.

It is generally recognized that when we bottle up our emotions, and when we are unable to express our emotion-laden thoughts, we build up harmful tension, and in some cases create concealed complexes.

Sometimes it seems imperative to give vent to adverse emotions. But when we feel it is essential to release our pent-up emotions, we should be fully aware that what we are doing is, from other points of view, quite wrong, and we should try to keep matters within bounds.

In one paradoxically-sounding way, it might almost be said that it is better to do wrong mindfully than to do right mindlessly. Anything we do habitually without thinking we do mindlessly, and whether by other standards it is right or wrong is less important than the lack of mindfulness.

Mindfulness, Our First Requisite

Most of us are ordinary people and not supermen, so we often fail to prevent the operation of wrong will-activity, usually because at the time when we most need to make the effort, outer circumstances and our lack of mindfulness combine to make us forget to do so. The fault then, is not that our effort of will is unsuccessful, but that there is no effort at all. And so mindfulness is our first requisite in all aspects of the meditation way, because only by mindfulness can we be aware of the need for mental effort.

Time and again, while sincerely trying to rid our minds of delusion, greed, or hate in their many forms, we find that in various subtle ways they have gained a foothold before we have recognized them for what they are. Then it is necessary to subdue them as well as we can. This is the second great effort of will required on our way.

Wholesome Elements of the Mind

Preventing adverse mind states from arising, and subduing them when they have arisen is still only part of the picture. Such endeavours must be carried on side by side with the effort to arouse the wholesome elements of the mind, for their operation builds up reaction forces that lead to happiness and our furtherance on the road to liberation.

Though we may succeed in arousing a wholesome mind state for a time, the pressure of external circumstances and weight of adverse habits may combine to bring its operation to a standstill. We slip back into old ruts, old ways of thinking and acting.

Therefore it is necessary to exert an effort of will to keep wholesome mind states functioning as well as to arouse them in the first place. This effort to nurture and maintain wholesome mental elements when aroused is the third great effort.

The foregoing clear-cut distinction among the three great efforts is of course an artificial one and not an actual one, since each of the three efforts, in general, have to be carried out along with one or more of the others.

So when we try to prevent or suppress an adverse mind factor, we often do so by trying to arouse and maintain a wholesome one of more or less opposite nature.

For example, if we try to prevent or suppress some form of greed within ourselves, we try at the same time to arouse and maintain an unselfish mind factor such as generosity.

Delusion and Discernment

With the opposite factors of delusion and discernment it is the same. Our efforts to raise our minds out of the state of delusion are essentially the same as the efforts to cultivate that form of discernment the final aim of which is to penetrate to the true nature of things.

Intellectual tranquillity is the calm, smooth operation of the thought processes, while tranquillity of consciousness, or if you like, consciousness of tranquillity, is an even, unruffled awareness of all that arises with the mind. Tranquillity in both forms is essential, for its own sake, and also because its cultivation helps to destroy remorse. Remorse is a form of discontent or worry related to the guilt complex and its consequent unrest.

Mental Agility

Development of mental agility is also essential if the mind is to make progress in any direction, mundane or supermundane, and this applies to both intellectual agility and agility of consciousness, the latter being the ability to become quickly aware of the true significance of a situation and its implications. Both aspects of mental agility help to break down apathy and mental laziness.

The quality of mental resilience, in intellectual function and as a quality of consciousness, gives one the capacity to learn and unlearn, to examine new ideas, and to break down that inflexibility which accompanies wishful thinking and belief, and the dogmatism often associated with conceit.

Such mind factors as tranquillity, mental agility and resilience, compassion, and so forth never 'just happen'. They have to be consciously developed.

When we become aware of the need to break adverse habits we also realize our need for increased mindfulness and our lack of it. This is because the mechanical nature of our responses is so marked that our habitual reactions are completed before we have fully realized their nature or implications.

Commonplace Irritations

We have all suffered from commonplace irritations such as when we are talking to someone and another person has intruded to divert our companion's attention. Or we may have been waiting in a queue, and someone has inconsiderately 'jumped' it. Irritations in the traffic conditions of today are frequent.

In such situations, we may on examination find our inner reaction to be the same; a 'boiling-up' inside, perhaps followed by an angry or sarcastic remark justified, we feel, by the circumstances.

However, the point is that the initial inner feeling of anger in such cases is a mechanical or automatic surge of feeling, and therefore uncontrolled. The spoken remark is not mechanical, but has had to be formulated from thought. In the case of the sarcastic retort, it may even be a display of ready, quick wit.

Although the feeling of uncontrolled anger, aversion, or hatred which has spontaneously arisen may appear to be justified by ordinary standards, it is never really justified to one who is trying to reach the distant shore of ego-lessness and tranquillity.

The process of self-control is difficult to achieve because we are habitually conditioned to allowing our adverse mind states to gain considerable momentum. But we must remember that constant expression of adverse thoughts nurtures them to greater strength to the point where they may actually dominate our minds.

The Habit of Complaint

The usual way in which most of us express our adverse emotional states is by indulging in the habit of complaint.

We may complain about the weather, the inadequacies of other people, or the rising cost of living. No doubt we believe that such complaints are justified, but we are really missing the point. The point is that too often we complain mindlessly and merely as an automatic release for our adverse emotional states.

If on the other hand, we complain mindfully, and our complaints have a purpose and are meant to bring about a result, and if we are conscious of the purpose, then it is a different matter. Unthinking and habitual complaint is bad, if only for the reason that it *is* unthinking and habitual.

Lack of Self-discipline

While there may be no conscious volition about our negative attitudes and activities, and while we may not wilfully become impatient or angry, we merely allow the mood to happen.

In the same way, although we might not wilfully divert our attention from its proper object, we merely allow it, through lack of self-discipline, to wander.

Similarly too, having no real point to our habitual complaints, we complain simply as an outlet for ill-feeling. The lack of volition in all these things is, in the long term, as damaging to us as wrongly-directed volition would be.

Feeling an adverse emotion, we usually want to give vent to it, to say something spiteful, unkind, or harsh. But when we feel impelled to raise our voice in anger, we should try to speak quietly. When we feel a tendency to turn away without speaking, we should instead make an effort to reply calmly.

Egotistical Desire

In just the same way, when we become aware of the egotistical desire to express our own cleverness, importance, or wit, or if we feel hurt at being left out of the conversation, when we feel that our importance or even our existence is not recognized, we experience an urge to make our presence felt. This may be done by offering a joke or some trivial remark.

But by the cultivation of mindfulness we become aware of our egotism and learn to deal with it. Then we learn to speak when we have something to say, and make our jocular remarks to give pleasure to others rather than to show how witty we can be. Otherwise we refuse our ego its habitual self-gratification.

Although in one sense nothing is perfectly accomplished by the will alone, and all perfect achievements result from a kind of spontaneous and effortless activity, the apparent contradiction is resolved when we remember that before this perfect and spontaneous and effortless activity is attained, there is usually a long period of imperfect, deliberate, and effortful activity, with attendant disappointments, discouragements, and setbacks.

We can sow our seeds of self-discipline, but we then have to tend them and encourage a climate in which they can grow.

CHAPTER TWELVE

THE DEVELOPMENT OF WISDOM AND COMPASSION

Liberation of the mind is based upon the two qualities of wisdom and compassion. To develop compassion or love, we must have patience. Patience itself must develop in two ways, towards unpleasant and painful feelings, and towards other people. We must be able to observe the meanness, the mediocrity, and the selfishness of other people without becoming personally or emotionally involved.

When we have reduced or eliminated our own cravings through meditation, and when we stop projecting into other people the unsolved problems we do not want to face in ourselves, or the unfulfilled ideals which we have failed to realize in ourselves, we begin to gain understanding. Only then do we discard our pet ideas on how other individuals should behave, because we can inquire dispassionately into their motives and actions.

In understanding others, we can see when they are not aware of what they are doing, or if they are under the control of unhealthy tendencies which they do not comprehend. Knowing this, we can feel compassion for them.

Justice and Objectivity

To have compassion and patience implies a sense of justice and of objectivity. Without a sense of justice you cannot feel compassion. Objectivity is the seeing of things as they really are. It is non-greed, non-hatred, and non-delusion.

This unbiased and unemotional way of looking at things is not fully possible unless we have first gained a fair amount of self-knowledge and self-control, thereby transçending that unconscious state of existence in which most people live.

Our complexes, our unconscious processes of projection, compensation, and repression, colour our perceptions. Unless we become aware of this whole process and can at least temporarily discard it, we cannot hope to see things as they really are.

We also find after practising sincere analysis of our own motives, actions, words, and thoughts, that we can stand criticism much better, because we no longer resentfully close our eyes to the shadow side of our own character

How to Gain Objectivity

An effective way towards gaining such objectivity is to consider oneself not as 'I', but rather as 'a person'. In ordinary speech and writing the use of the word 'I' is obviously necessary, but someone with self-awareness will know what the 'I' really is. The royal and editorial prerogative of 'we' is slightly akin to such a form of thinking, with its suggestion that there is some considered opinion being stated.

Once you have succeeded in objectivity you cannot be hurt in the old way by what others do or say to you, because you are a controlled personality instead of being a tender egocentricity of self-attachment.

It is best, in thought at least, not to consider that

'I have a body', but rather that 'there is a body', not my body or someone else's body but just 'there is a body'. This can be applied in any case where there is identification, such as, instead of 'I hear something', one would think, 'there is sound'.

The habit of thinking promotes an inner objectivity, and thus weakens the inclination towards both aversion and conceit, allowing one to bear patiently ridicule, contempt, or the arrogance of others.

Genuine progress towards liberation is inevitably connection with emptying the mind of all those pursuits, views, and inclinations which bind it to self-attachment. You cannot be broken, despondent, despairing or crushed, if there is nothing there to be broken. It has been said that to abide in the realm of non-self is to live in the abode of great men.

Sensual Escapism

Sometimes when painful, unpleasant feelings arise, a person who is unable to endure them tries to escape into a pursuit of sensual pleasure to get away from the suffering.

Unfortunately this is no real solution to the problem because the person then has to cope with problems inherent in sensual escapism. On the other hand, the escape may take the form of irritation and aversion to others, 'taking it out on other people' in fact.

These methods are no answer, because all that has happened has been an attempt to switch the attention from one's suffering on to something else. And once again the inability to endure suffering has been strengthened. Also strengthened has been the tendency to run away, and a futile resistance to the unpleasant. The inclination to sensuality or mental dissipation has been promoted too, and the inclination to dislike or hate others.

This is typical of a person who is unable to investigate and understand his problems and difficulties. He runs away from them and then becomes dependent on the escapes, thus constantly multiplying his problems and difficulties.

True patience is the capacity to endure unpleasant sensations, whether caused by another or not, and not to be in despair about them but to realize they are impermanent, and consequently void and empty.

Freedom from Inner Conflicts

To have love and compassion for others there must be freedom from inner conflicts and an absence of pride, conceit, and self-centredness. There must be inner harmony and clarity of understanding.

Conceit is one of the greatest hindrances to compassion. If one possesses a high idea of oneself and is unable to live up to it, a feeling of inner inferiority results, which is often compensated for by delusions of superiority, and one's own self-dislike is projected on to other people.

It is to be emphasized that a person who progresses on the path to wisdom should neither praise himself for his achievements nor look with contempt on those who have not reached the same state. This is important because it implies the getting rid of all our prejudices, class and otherwise.

The attitude implies that we should cease to condemn other people for their moral and intellectual weaknesses, and implies that we become aware of their good and healthy sides, even if these are small and undeveloped. We should feel compassion for their shortcomings if we are in the position of knowing that no one can escape the results of their previous actions.

Advantages of Solitude

The greater the freedom from the hindrances of self, the better we are prepared to establish stillness of mind and intuitive insight, and these qualities gained, we can further develop progressive stages of meditation. With increasing insight and understanding one feels more and more inclination for solitude and contemplation.

Schopenhauer once said that solitude has two advantages; firstly that one is with oneself, and secondly that one is not together with others.

The more you see the necessity for developing awareness and meditation, love and compassion, the less you are afraid of being alone. You may even come to consider the gregarious instinct and the liking for discussion a hindrance, or as an escape from your main task of liberating yourself from desire and confusion. To find joy in solitude is one of the delights brought about through meditation and insight.

Opinions of Others

Another aspect of being alone is that you cease to seek self-affirmation and affection and become more and more unconcerned about the opinions others hold of you.

You learn to maintain equanimity whether they praise or blame you, whether they feel contempt for you, or whether they respect you, whether they speak well or ill about your friends, or whether they act in a stupid, mean, or selfish way.

One has to learn to be able to observe all of this and feel neither gladness nor aversion. Only then is one inwardly independent, because aversion is just as binding as attachment.

Once all selfish desire has been eliminated, one is alone with the strength of reality, no longer needing artificial props for an ego, for the ego has been discovered, analysed, and controlled. Everywhere and under all circumstances one is alone. But as long as one is attached to something, however subtly, one is not alone in this sense of knowing reality.

Lasting Freedom

When meditation has been practised through the first stage of investigation and reflection, to the second stage where discursive thinking comes to an end and happiness is maintained and stillness of mind is strengthened, then on to the third stage in which elation is abandoned and equanimity, mindfulness and clear comprehension are discovered, and finally on to the fourth stage where all other states are transcended, then comes lasting freedom.

Concentration and awareness never leave a person thus enlightened, whether he is walking, standing, sitting, or lying down. He does not fidget with his hands or feet, or twitch his body or face. He is not incoherent in speech or confused in his senses, for there is no agitation left in mind or body.

The constant demeanour of such a person is one of contentment, both in private and in public. He is frugal and of good life and habits. In a crowd he stands apart, always even and unchanged. In gain or in loss he is neither elated nor cast down.

This sounds like a tall order of perfection, and it is just that. Yet it is the state which everyone desires, at least in part, from time to time. To relate such perfection is also to mirror the opposites, the imperfections. And who wants to be imperfect?

Only by rising above the conflicts of duality can the perfection of unity be achieved.

Reading No Substitute for Practice

As has been stated elsewhere in this book, reading

by itself is no substitute for practice. Some people do not go on practising regularly, but continue reading for all they are worth, sometimes without reflecting sufficiently over what they have read.

Reading is easy when compared with meditation or reflection, which may initially entail a strenuous mental effort. Meditation can be difficult at the beginning, just as doing anything new is difficult. But if we persevere and get the right ideas behind it, it becomes easy and interesting.

Blind theoretical acceptance is no substitute for the arrival at practical conclusions for oneself. The true teacher always tries to demonstrate either by analogy, practical application, or example. Such a lesson is better remembered by the student than if he is merely told something, yet not allowed to pursue the fact from cause to result. A layman can read from a chemistry textbook that water is made up of hydrogen and oxygen. He can just accept the fact, and even try to visualize the action of the two gases. But if he could learn how to analyse water and detect the gases, go into a laboratory and do the analysis correctly, then he would have satisfactory practical knowledge of the composition of water.

Laboratory of the Mind

Clearly there is much of knowledge which we have to take on the word of others, since we lack the time and the ability to make our own tests. Concerning meditation however, there is no need to accept the findings of others.

Teachers can only point the way, and the practical application is there for the student to discover. He then becomes his own teacher. The great scientists think over problems in their minds, trying to find solutions which are then verified by practical experiments.

In meditation, the mind is the laboratory in which we can experiment with our ideas and attitudes, and when the solutions are revealed we can apply them practically to life.

The power of insight-knowledge is not obtainable for ordinary human beings using 'normal' consciousness. The minds of most men in the ordinary way are incapable of penetrating insight or of comprehending fully the exact nature of things.

As a rule comprehension power is limited, and so are all the other faculties with which man is equipped. He can see and know only those things which come to him through the channels of his sense organs, eyes, ears, and so forth.

Therefore man usually thinks that he cannot believe or know anything except through the sense organs. What he frequently does not realize is that his human powers as such are limited, and he imagines that he is content with his direct and inductive knowledge.

Latent Powers

Yet man by nature possesses powers which are latent, and he can rise very much higher than his usual standards. In order to obtain such powers one has to exercise and practise concentration.

To obtain strong concentration of mind is the first and hardest task to be accomplished, for the mind is difficult to control in the beginning. It seeks apparent delight here and there, and the way to curb this factor is by paying attention to one's conduct.

Desire is the paramount motivating element in the ordinary mind, for it creates, precedes, and dominates one's action. Such uncontrolled desire obviously hinders progress in concentration, just as do ill-will, laziness, distraction, worry, and perplexity. When these factors are prohibited, one has won the first stage in the practice of meditation.

Two Forms of Concentration

A similar statement has been made earlier in this book, and the object is not repetition, but rather to emphasize the distinction between mere intellectual concentration and the higher concentration necessary to meditation.

This distinction existing between the two forms of concentration should not be lost sight of in the study of the subject, because to the fresh student it is likely to give rise to some confusion.

Anybody engaged upon a task needs to focus his attention on the matter in hand, but this ordinary kind of concentration cannot be said to overcome ill-will, worry, and so forth, which is the case with the higher kind of concentration required in meditation. A person succeeding in the higher concentration of meditation practice is not in a state of mental bondage, his mind being freed from usual attachment and considerations.

This higher concentration of mind is undistracted because it is defined as that one-pointedness arising from freedom from ill-will and all the other mundane desires and feelings. In such successful meditation the mind soars above the lower nature.

So the difference between ordinary intellectual concentration and the higher form is that in ordinary concentration the mind still holds all the unwholesome aspects of its own creation, whereas the higher form is devoid of them.

The Reality of Life

If a person has not entered into meditation, he has missed the reality of life, for without it there can be no true knowledge. But meditation does not come from another, but can only be attained by one's own exertion and concentration. Yet no amount of practice will be of any use if one's moral character is constantly being tainted.

But the practice itself does good and increasingly helps the sincere student to avoid evil. Repeated meditation alone will bring purity and calmness of mind. The faculty of bringing back to steadfastness a wandering mind is each time a step in the progress.

There are people who will never meditate because they are afraid of perceiving too clearly the wretchedness of their own present position of futility. Others are quite content to blindly follow the lead of someone, or some doctrine, in which they have placed their trust.

Such people, with an unthinking and ingrained belief will bring forward arguments to rationalize their belief, and no amount of logic will move them from it, because they will ignore argument to the contrary.

All the stark materialism with its train of misery, folly, and error, is owing to the lack of proper understanding of one's true nature.

Behind the Sense Perceptions

Down through the ages there have been people who have maintained that the possibility exists for getting in touch with what is behind the sense perceptions. They are the mystics. They do not belong to any special race or religion and some of them have not belonged to any specific religion or school of philosophy at all.

All of these mystics have discovered a special non-rational experience in which they have attained some degree of illumination or insight into the essential and normally hidden nature of reality.

This knowledge of essential nature is not abstract

like intellectual 'knowing'. It is as concrete as any sense experience. There comes an immediate assurance of a unity lying behind the senses, which is as real as one's own existence.

This knowledge, when realized, has such a quality of conviction that it can never afterwards be doubted. The person experiencing it does not 'feel', he knows. He knows that he has made a connection with the reality behind appearances, and that he is enabled to renew this extraordinary experience from time to time.

Since quite obviously such an illumination will alter the tenor of one's life for the better, broadening its aspect, no one should shy away from the consideration of such an experience. When success crowns the practice of meditation, the future conduct is irradiated by the experience.

The 'new' man is able to overcome his troubles with fortitude and joy. He behaves with increased sincerity, wisdom, and courage, and with a new devotion to his living. The capacity for delight and appreciation is increased, and even his sense perceptions reveal a fresh significance in ordinary phenomenal things.

Mystical Experience Is Common
There is no need to dismiss such claims as fantastic delusions, not only because there is a basic likeness amongst the accounts given by different people about the experience, but also because mystical experience is much more common than is generally imagined.

We all have mystical experiences to a greater or lesser degree in our lifetime. These 'spontaneous' experiences are not necessarily led up to by any form of discipline, prayer, or contemplation, but usually occur when we are in surroundings of great natural beauty, or when we have momentarily uncovered a selfless form of thinking which we recognize as being greater than our usual way of thought. No particular state of mind or body may precede these experiences, and many people brush them aside as being meaningless.

Yet if these experiences which apparently 'come out of the blue' in any way catch the attention forcefully, there is a double effect. First of all they leave us with a slightly more reflective attitude to life thereafter, and secondly they enable us to recognize a similar experience when recounted by someone else.

For although such experiences are often found difficult to describe, an account, however falteringly given, speaks instantly to the person who has also had such an experience.

The great poets, musicians, and painters have had mystical experiences quite naturally. Wordsworth, Browning, Whitman, have all recounted them. Beethoven, Bach, and Franck have expressed them beautifully in their musical creations. El Greco and others have painted them.

Tennyson's Meditation Experiences

One could quote many examples of the expression of meditation experiences. Here is just one from Tennyson: '... out of the intensity of the consciousness of individuality, the individuality itself seemed to dissolve and fade away into boundless being; and this is not a confused state, but the clearest of the clearest, the surest of the surest, the weirdest of the weirdest, utterly beyond words - where death was an almost laughable impossibility - the loss of personality (if so it were) seeming no extinction, but the only true life. I am ashamed of my feeble description. Have I not said the state is utterly beyond words?'

Tennyson frequently enjoyed such experiences.

On reading such accounts, it is always found that there is a fundamental agreement that behind all phenomena is an underlying unity. Sometimes an account may be coloured by the society or the environment to which the writer belongs, but there is always the basic agreement of the discovery of unity.

Good poetry is permeated with imagery and inner meanings expressing mystical experience. Such insight from meditation is of the mind, not of matter.

The discovery of unity has been called by many names. Some have called it God, others have called it the Absolute, World-Soul, Love, or Wisdom. This has been due to the attempt to express the inexpressible in common terms by use of the restrictions of words.

Purity of Motive
Those who wish to meditate should for their own benefit try to answer to themselves as honestly as possible the questions: 'Why do I wish to meditate?' – 'What do I wish to gain by it?' or 'What is my aim as regards my own life, my own development?' This is essential before one starts to meditate, for the foundation of meditation is purity of motive.

If the aim of the meditator is not a lofty one, if he only wants to 'find out all about it' out of mere curiosity, or if he wishes to attain insight into the minds of his fellow men in order to increase his own worldly success, greed being the motive in this case, he will not succeed and will give up his attempts during the first stage.

There are some exceptions who are able to correct their wrong approach to meditation by growing in understanding during the course of the practice. Mainly however, the pre-requisite is sincerity, and the exceptions quickly discover their own underlying honesty.

Purity of motive or mind, as far as the ordinary person can understand it, is obedience to one's conscience, to the so-called inner voice, which tells one what is right and what is wrong.

Emptying Thoughts from the Mind

The beginning of meditation is the process of emptying thoughts from the mind. In a sense it is impossible not to think but there are two different ways of thought. The first is our ordinary way of thinking, that is to think *ABOUT* things from a personal point of view, to judge in accordance with our own ideas of what is wrong and right, to search for a reason, an excuse, an explanation, to compare, to lose oneself in memories, to speculate about the future, and so forth.

All this and every other type of thinking on similar lines is usually referred to as 'considering' thought the term is inadequate. This 'considering' is a great obstacle to meditation, and while it lasts meditation is made impossible.

The second way of thinking is only to observe and only to register a chosen object, the object by itself, without any 'surrounding' so to speak, and without giving way to any thought of the considering type which might arise. This and this alone is the right function of the meditator. It should be practised whenever possible, even when not actually sitting down to one's stated time given over to meditation.

This mindfulness is of paramount importance for the attainment of insight. At this point the aim is to make quite clear the fundamental difference between ordinary thought, which constantly oscillates between the past and the future, and mindfulness or concentration, which is always in the present.

A Beginner's Difficulties

To give an illustration of difficulties which might beset a beginner, a person might sit down to meditate at a time when everything seems quiet. Suddenly a dog howls, then a radio is switched on, and later the sound of footsteps is heard.

If one registers each of these noises by naming and thinking about them, one will immediately get caught up in a labyrinth of uncontrolled thoughts and emotions.

The howl of the dog may lead to pity for the animal and the assumption that someone has hurt it, or to thoughts of anger. If a pleasant melody comes from the radio one may enjoy it for the moment and forget that one wishes to meditate.

Memories of the past may arise. If any of these things seem unpleasant, one may become angry. The footsteps may make one curious as to whom they belong, and so on.

Thinking in the second way however, one does not observe and register the howl of the dog, the noise of the radio, or the footsteps. One observes and registers only the most outstanding function of the body at that moment, under the circumstances described, namely that of hearing.

Holding on with a certain amount of gentle intensity to the observing and registering of hearing, one is no longer disturbed. Nor does one get angry, feel frustrated in the attempt to meditate, or think about what has happened or might have happened or will happen.

In fact, one has achieved the beginning of mindfulness. One lives no longer in the past or in the future, one is in the present.

The Way to Success

This method of overcoming difficulties is the way to success in meditation. It can be applied equally to any other sensation besides that of hearing. When the sensation, hearing or whatever, has been controlled in the way described, that sensation is rendered harmless, and the meditation can proceed uninterrupted.

The adept can, if he wishes, transfer his concentration to such phenomena, making it the 'object' of his meditation. This requires mastery however, and the beginner is advised to merely 'notice' the phenomena in passing, neither desiring it nor rejecting it. It will not then impede the meditation practice as described in Chapter Eight.

Meditation alone is not a religion in the sense in which that word is commonly understood, for it is not a system of faith and worship. Indeed, mere belief is dethroned and is substituted by confidence based on knowledge. In that, it may be said that meditation is the main requirement of true religion.

Nor is meditation something merely to be preserved in books, or a subject to be studied from a historical or literary point of view. On the contrary it is to be learnt and put into practice in the course of one's daily life, for without practice one cannot appreciate its truth. Meditation is to be studied, and more to be practised, and above all to be realized. Self-realization is its ultimate goal.

We are people passing through the human school, and our task is to bring forth *MIND* from our central essence of the self, and evolve it up to its highest capacity.

CHAPTER THIRTEEN

IN SEARCH OF TRUTH

The growth of interest in meditation must be obvious to any observer of the trend of thought. A true meditator is a pioneer in search of truth, a compassionate and tolerant pioneer seeking to disarm but one enemy. The name of that enemy is Ignorance.

His own free intelligence leads the meditator to the recompense of supreme knowledge and insight. And since meditation is not an imposed dogma it invites the free investigation of reason to guide each one upon its path.

The subject for meditation is best if it is one which really interests the student, for he must become absorbed in it to the degree that the idea will soon lead to one-pointedness of mind.

When the attention has been concentrated and the subject for meditation has been thoroughly examined and analysed, the student should reflect upon all he has learned through his analysis.

Plane of Pure Thought

It is following upon this that intuitive thinking will begin to function. Then a sense of happiness and well-being is experienced, by the student, and he is aware that he is approaching the plane of pure thought.

Soon he is able to discard all the thoughts which might be described as 'verbal'. He will no longer need these word thoughts, for intuition alone will allow him to contact his subject. In other words, the meditator and his subject have become identified.

In this way are the subtler and superior states of consciousness achieved.

Calm, penetrating thoughts acquired during meditation will last for some time, the length of time increasing with practice. The student should, and more than likely will anyway, keep in his mind all that he has experienced during the meditation. The cultivated habit of observation makes concentration easier all the time.

Modification of Ideas

The experience of meditation will gradually but repeatedly cause the student to modify and change his ideas. The best rule here is to follow that which seems to be true at that given moment.

Another guideline is the simple ethical one of asking whether a thought or act will increase or diminish the suffering of oneself, or of any other being. The honest answering of such a question furthers the arousing of the healthy, wholesome elements of the mind.

The mind must remain free of wrong thought, guilt, or any other hindrance to its freedom to accept the new ideas which the intelligence will perceive as it is increasingly purified by meditation. It must never become the slave of habits of thought.

In studying meditation it is essential to have understood the ideas of the teaching. As previously stated, meditation imposes no dogmas. The aim is for a reasoned, uncluttered thinking process. 'Faith' must here follow the dictates of reason. The student who has grasped this idea becomes in time his own guide, from that knowledge which is within himself.

His present vision has been determined by the tendencies, the characteristics, and the nature of thoughts he has created in the past. Any future vision will likewise be created by the thoughts and actions of the present. It has to be stressed again that ignorance decreases as thought is purified.

Life Is Dynamic

Life can be re-created, and the level of consciousness can be raised, because life is itself not static, but dynamic. It follows then that in any aspects of personality, taken separately or collectively, there is nothing unchangeable, nothing permanent, nothing finally which can be called 'self'. The full realization of this can be gained through meditation. It is because change or renewal is possible that we can modify our own nature and improve it.

There is, due to ignorance and prejudice, some doubt amongst many people as to the validity of meditation. To such minds it is allied to various forms of extreme asceticism, or even self-mortification of a kind abhorrent to most.

To many Western people asceticism is tied up with ideas of mortification of the flesh, and with a somewhat painful renunciation of the world, and indeed the word ascetic was first applied to those earlier Christians who practised flagellation as a means to salvation or an attempt by those weighed down by the guilt of original sin to become reconciled with their Creator.

Something Lacking

Yet even in its welfare state glory the West has not yet managed to provide universal joy. Political argument has not resolved the question of human happiness. People are never totally satisfied, even when all their physical needs are catered for. There is always something lacking, some undefined need which cannot be met by however much material comfort is afforded.

To overcome these ills it is necessary to reassess our values. Although material things in life are undoubtedly important, the possession of them does not solve all our problems or make us complete. Assuming that we have looked after our physical needs, there still remains the question of our attitudes, our thinking processes, which at times will give us a profound sense of dissatisfaction.

Mental questioning of the 'reason' for our being is the simplest and most obvious evidence for the existence of another 'self' which can question the significance of our lives. An even greater simplification is the application of the logical response of 'how do I find out?'

To remain on this simplistic level, the answer would then be to go to that part of the mind which is capable of promoting the initial question about our outer life. This in turn again poses the question of how.

Superiority of Eastern System

It is at this point that we find that the East is ahead of the West in the matter. All the religious systems have their orthodoxies of restraint, moralities, lofty ideals, procedures, practices, and hierarchies, and even in some cases a negative resignation to fate.

Let it be understood that the above is not intended as a denigration of any, or all, religions. The prohibitions to ensure moral living cannot be condemned.

Yet only in certain systems of the Far East is there to be found a light shed upon the actual and practical technique of spiritual aspiration. Few other great historical traditions allow us to isolate the elements of meditation so easily as do the writings of the East.

The methods are there for developing the inner force without accessories of mind impulse, such as religious suggestion or raptures. Thus meditation is raised to the full dignity of an impersonal science, without trappings.

The 'Reflex Image' Explained

In Stage Four of this book, in Chapter Eight, under the heading: 'Placing the Mind on the State of Absorption', I have referred to the 'reflex image'. Since the first publication of the book I have had several queries as to what precisely is meant by a 'reflex image'. The explanation is as follows.

When the third stage has been mastered, an 'image' will appear in a few days. As stated in Stage Four, this image will vary from person to person.

Perhaps the simplest analogy is to ask the student to look at a brightly lit electric light bulb or the sun, and then to look away. For a few seconds before the vision is back to normal, the student will see an image of the light for a few seconds, due to contraction of the pupil.

It must be emphasized that this is merely analogous, since the reflex image in meditation is only a 'mental' image, unless, of course, the student has been practising some technique involving a bright light.

The Eye Within

In the method of meditation described in this book, the reflex image serves as a basis for concentration, but it first has to be established in such a way that one continues to 'see' it even involuntarily, with the eyes closed or open. It is not the physical eye that fixes the gaze, but the eye that has been opened within. The procedure for meditation remains the same as before, and one has to identify oneself with the mental image, forgetting everything else, just as was done previously with the 'image' provided by the physical sense.

If the concentration on the new interior image is properly carried out, a new reflex, something purer still, without form or colour, finally springs out from it. Here again, to try and anticipate questions, the writer on meditation is faced with the difficulty of attempting to describe the indescribable.

All that can be said is that this new reflex image resembles the dissipation of a fog, or the appearance of a moon appearing from behind clouds. These attempted descriptions are again only analogous, and it has to be remembered that the only way to discover what it is really like is to practice and gain for oneself.

Any person who is making real progress in meditation has no need of asking such questions as they belong to the mundane aspect of existence. I emphasized in Stage Four that it is unhelpful to tell a student what phenomena might occur in the higher stages of meditation, as this could lead to accusations of suggestion.

All that can usefully be done is to give guidance as to method, but the discoveries must be those of the individual.

Colour and Light Phenomena

Before going any further it would be as well to forestall any misunderstandings arising from implications of what seem to some a form of almost hypnotic technique.

It is possible that some people, seeking for short cuts to reach the supersensible without too much effort, may believe they have found something of the sort in the colour and light phenomena. They might then mistakenly believe that by practising forms of hypnosis they can dispense with any kind of renunciation, discipline, or spiritual effort.

This would be a grave mistake. What ought to be remembered is that these initial procedures mean very little in themselves. Their purpose is merely to neutralize peripheral sensitivity. Then it is a question of seeing firstly if anything of 'consciousness' still remains after neutralization has been achieved, and then, if it has, what experience may result.

It is well known to occultists that procedures involving colour and light phenomena have been used by visionaries and by magicians, and also in certain forms of experimental hypnotism. Bright light gazing, magic mirror gazing, and other ways of using a luminous point to acquire a mediumistic or foretelling result, have long been practised.

These forms of self-hypnosis are best left alone. They can, if persisted in, bring forth complexes of all kinds. These may become projected, resulting in visions which can become extremely dangerous.

For our present purpose such practices are useless, being either neutral or, at worst, distracting. Since they do not go beyond individuality and can only lead to the opening up of the manifestation of obscure influences, they are to be avoided. The path of meditation is one that leaves all such psychic dross far behind.

First Condition for Effective Use

For the effective use of the reflex image the first condition is that the consciousness should be concentrated and detached and able to maintain itself by its own efforts. Then, when peripheral sensitivity is neutralized, it is possible to go 'up' rather than down, the aim being to progress rather than to sink into the morass of the lower grades of mediumship.

The object is to obtain a purified super consciousness. Spiritual tension imbued with the idea of awakening is needed, the mind acting like a compressed spring on the point of release. Given these prerequisite conditions, the aspirant can go beyond the act of concentration on the reflex image, absorbing it and thus transcending it.

Throughout the practice of meditation one is simply creating, relatively quickly and conveniently, conditions which favour a further action presupposing a higher development of consciousness.

What is ultimately being sought is a fundamental orientation of the spirit, a reintegration with that which has been 'lost'. Activism, and perhaps many other 'isms' have extended to all walks and conditions of life, to absorb life in their tumults and agitations until they have come to be seen as life itself. The 'being' aspect of life has been overcome by the 'becoming' aspects of life, even on the cultural plane.

It is futile to suppose that we can react against this situation, except in intellectual terms. The causes of the modern dilemma are too remote and complex to be dealt with in the short term. Yet success for the individual is possible, for he can become qualified to deal with the world in which he finds himself, and the affirmation of such a vision is particularly necessary today.

Values of Meditation

To return to the values of meditation, it can be said that it can lead to a new life formation, orientated to the 'after-material', and will show what mastery and real action are to those who know only action in its obscure and irrational forms.

In its affirming of pure transcendency as a detachment both in action and beyond action, meditation can ensure a firmness which cannot be disturbed or overthrown by the changeable. Forces are radiated which are beneficial to an astonishing degree, and which can act upon destinies untold.

Those who have reached an unconditioned state of being are thereby freed to make their own conditions on life by will alone. Such accomplished ones have no need of dogmas, 'religious' aids, mysticism and any confused kind, manias for occult phenomena, or for contaminations of psychoanalysis, or for spiritual deviations of any sort.

It is unfortunately the case that certain self-interested groups who claim to have gained a monopoly of profane truth do their best to pile discredit upon ideals and wisdom which have always been known as the culminating point of any civilization.

This is rather like the bad salesman who tries to sell one car by denigrating another make. What the customer really wants to know is about the car he is considering, not the defects of another vehicle.

Modern man not only has to fight against materialism, he also has to defend himself against the traps of false supernaturalism. He will be firmly effective if he can return to the origins, assimilate the ancient traditions, and is capable of re-establishing his inner condition.

The Sense of 'I'

The ordinary man is not really all that far above the animal in point of consciousness. Certainly he has the faculty of reason, but his sense of 'I' is mainly a matter of the wants of the body, the satisfaction of appetites, the securing of personal comforts, and the gratifications of passions, even the expression of lust and power. This is only so in varying degrees of course, but for such a person to speak of 'my mind' or 'my soul' would be from a position below, and not from the position of knowledge of any real self.

But that man has advanced in culture who can see that above himself there are higher attributes. He is only satisfied with more refined things, whereas the less cultured man is easily satisfied with the more material and gross sense gratifications. Yet even the highly cultivated are only experiencing a more refined form of sense gratification.

But this 'advanced' man begins to have a higher conception of the 'I', when he uses his mind to pass on to the mental plane of intellect. He then begins to feel that there is something within him that is much higher than the mere physical plane, and he discovers that his mind often seems more real to him than the body, and that when he is deeply concentrated in thought or study he has the ability to almost forget its existence.

Here it is that new difficulties emerge, for his mind thinks of problems which demand an answer. As soon as he thinks he has answered a problem, it offers itself up in a new phase, and he then has to seek an explanation for that. For the mind, even when not controlled by the will, has a wonderful range, and so the man travels around in a mental circle, constantly confronted by the unknown.

This is perplexing and disturbing, particularly as the man is probably well read and has attained a good deal of knowledge. A man of little knowledge and understanding does not appear to be aware of the existence of so many of these problems of our 'advanced' man, and cannot appreciate the tortured uneasiness of his counterpart.

Happy Pig or Unhappy Philosopher?

It is a state of affairs in which the 'advanced' man is likely to ask himself questions such as 'is it better to be a happy pig, or an unhappy philosopher?' He knows that he has advanced, but even so, his 'I' does not provide the answer to his perplexities.

Such men frequently become pessimists, seeing life as disappointing and a curse rather than a blessing; a pointless, futile existence.

The man on the physical plane, who is absorbed solely in gratifying his animal nature, has few, if any, such disquieting thoughts. Nor does the man on the spiritual plane, for he knows that his mind is an instrument of himself, rather than as being himself.

Furthermore, the spiritual man knows that the mind is imperfect but that he has within himself the key to all knowledge. This ultimate knowledge is locked up within the ego, and the cultivated, trained mind, guided by the awakened will can unlock it, grasping it as it unfolds.

Thus the lower man is untroubled because of his ignorance, while the higher man is untroubled because of his knowledge. Most of us, of course, are somewhere between these two extremes.

When the 'advanced' man realizes this he can begin to render the implications as tangible and effective, and has no further need of despair. It is as though he had mastered and tamed a wild horse, and can henceforth direct the animal as he wishes.

When such a man has succeeded in passing from the mental plane into the spiritual plane he realizes that the 'I' is something higher than both body and mind and that both of the latter are used as instruments by the ego. He can then persist until he reaches a plane of 'egolessness' which cannot in any way be described in mundane terms.

Such knowledge is not gained by purely intellectual reasoning, although these efforts of mind are necessary to help in the unfolding of the knowledge. The real knowledge 'comes' however, as a special form of consciousness.

Self-Mastery
It is well at this point to include a reminder. The student has to master himself before he can hope to exert an influence beyond himself. There is no soft option, no overnight success story, each step has to be taken in turn, and by his own effort.

If the task sounds much too formidable, then abandon it before even starting. On the other hand it is better to accept the challenge, because meditation is beneficial even after only a short time. A really hungry person will not be too fussy about what he eats, but the false-appetited diner will only be bored by food.

After giving a lecture on meditation, I was approached by a member of the audience who said that it seemed too difficult for him. This was said in an almost accusing tone, as if I were withholding some secret of rapid success. I could only assure him that if he wished to meditate, then the best thing to do was to – meditate!

Life gives many of us an inferiority complex, among other complexes. To suggest that there are higher states of being induces in some people the reaction that if there are, then they can never reach them.

The secret is to relax, and begin. Don't anticipate too much, just see what happens. Find the best conditions you can in which to practise. If you feel a bit self-conscious and foolish the first two or three times, never mind, the feeling will pass as you slowly but surely progress.

Meditators are not 'Dreamy'

Some people are afraid that if they practise meditation they will end up by going about in a 'dreamy' fashion, in some sort of semi-trance state in which they are liable to be knocked down by a bus, or lose their jobs through inattention.

Remember instead that the state of meditation is entirely under the control of the will, and should be entered into only deliberately and at the proper times. The will must be master of this, as of every other mental state. Meditators are not 'day-dreamers', but men and women who have full control of themselves and their moods. Meditation is a system of awakening, of becoming aware, and not a way of putting oneself to sleep.

Another thing which impedes progress is the idea that one already knows something or everything about meditation because one has read all the available literature, and feels he has already had certain experiences and knows exactly what they mean. This is by no means an uncommon attitude and as long as it lasts the student is deadlocked and cannot progress. It is conceit rooted in delusion.

There is only one right attitude, and that is the wish to learn, to be determined to carry on. In other words, a complete surrender to the practice.

Freedom of the Spirit

When people talk of freedom, it might be as well for them to practice a little introspection on the subject. Given political freedom, civil freedom, social freedom, or any other kind, man is still not satisfied, desirable and useful though they might be, for the only kind of freedom which can perfectly satisfy him is the one he probably most neglects, the freedom of the spirit.

We come into life and grow up with the ideas and traditions other men have given us. This inheritance to some extent determines our environment, and the instincts we express become the property of others in a later generation.

Under the pressure of such uncertain and often confusing influences we feel compelled to think and act for or against ideologies, usually popularly presented. The confusion can become total because we have not developed three-dimensional thinking.

And there are times when life beats us down, and in anguish, pain, and tears, we look about helplessly and ask questions about life. Too often the answers are found to be outmoded or unwanted. At such times either discipline and personal control is asserted, or the repressed violence within man's instincts is released, to do great harm.

The Study of Behaviour

The modern approach man has taken to understand 'mind', is through the study of behaviour, and delving into those influences that deal with genealogy or parental contributions to our mental and physical make-up. Generally this aspect in education, like that of psychotherapy, aims largely at helping the mentally ill.

The average person is rarely under such scrutiny until he becomes either physically or mentally maladjusted. The new approach can be likened to preventive medicine which, when applied, can immunize the individual against mental upsets and emotional instability.

Properly understood, insight can present the way of mindfulness in a Western perspective to help with such problems. It can employ the best to be found in mental sciences to complement techniques used in effective meditative practice. In such a way a good synthesis can be realized for real advance in the cultural and spiritual life.

Compulsions

Today we are assaulted on every side by powerful psychological influences, so often born of the desire of others to control our movement and thought. We can be frightened by the effectiveness of such compulsions, which play upon the instincts and emotions. Our fears may be widened when we think about compulsion or conformity which destroys the creativeness in man.

We might be consoled when we reflect that the new sciences can be used for good or evil. Yet the trend to control human thinking continues in a compelling flood, and demanding ideologies rise and fall like waves of the sea.

It is the calmed mind alone which can deal with these problems that excite the instincts, and attachments that arise continually to remind us of our many limitations.

In meditation there is found time and

opportunity to rebuild one's outlook and to move closer to insight. On a large scale this could help to stop the further spread of emotional immaturity which threatens our new, rapidly changing world, in which the most thoughtful of men agree that many of our troubles can be traced to negative attachments and destructive instincts.

Solving Problems by Meditation

The meditation way then, can solve our problems only by attacking them at their origins, not at their surface manifestations, for they can be finally resolved in no other way.

The origin or root cause of all problems is ignorance, which is really a primal blindness that prevents us from discerning the true nature of existence; a basic ignorance that makes us seek outwardly for a permanent personal happiness in an unsatisfactory world of impermanence and illusion. It is this wrong will activity which builds up the reaction forces that repeatedly give rise to our suffering and unhappiness.

Finally, meditation is a matter of understanding, not of dialectical ability, but of inner illumination that comes of the growth from the lowly condition of mundane existence to the supernormal wisdom.

INDEX